HOLY GHOST PRIMER

Stepping into Communion
WITH
the Holy Spirit

Reed D. Tibbetts

HOLY GHOST PRIMER
© 2017 by Reed D. Tibbetts

Published by Insight International, Inc.
contact@freshword.com
www.freshword.com
918-493-1718

All rights reserved. No part of this book may be reproduced or transmitted in any form or by any means, electronic or mechanical, including photocopying and recording, or by an information storage and retrieval system, without permission in writing from the author.

All Scripture quotations, unless otherwise noted, are taken from the *New American Standard Bible®*, © 1960, 1962, 1963, 1968, 1971, 1972, 1973, 1975, 1977, 1995 by The Lockman Foundation. Used by permission.www.Lockman.org

Scripture quotation marked "KJV" is taken from the King James Version of the Bible.

ISBN: 978-1-943361-28-1
E-book ISBN: 978-1-943361-29-8

Library of Congress Control Number: 2016958590

Printed in the United States of America.

ENDORSEMENTS FOR *HOLY GHOST PRIMER*

"I have known my friend, Reed Tibbetts, for thirty-six years. I am convinced that Reed is a man of absolute integrity. He is a diligent student of the Bible. He is comfortable in his relationship with the Holy Spirit. I am anticipating further Biblical teachings from Reed Tibbetts."

—Richard C. Benjamin Sr.,
Apostle and Founding Pastor of
Abbott Loop Christian Center,
Anchorage, Alaska

"Reed serves faithfully and loyally as one of the elders in the church I pastor. He is one of the best theological minds I have had the privilege of calling my friend. His teachings are a unique mix of potent ingredients that form a special recipe of the truth, and reach the minds and spirits of those he teaches. Relax, receive, and enjoy the concepts of his latest book."

—Mike Connaway, Senior Pastor of
VLife Church, McKinney, Texas
and Author of *My Third House*

"Reed Tibbetts is one of the most preeminent theologians I have ever met. He brings his steeped knowledge of the Bible, and uses his God-given anointing, to write books that encourage and challenge all believers to grow in their relationship with God. Reed has a great ability to reach all generations in his writings and teachings. He is truly a man of God."

—Gabriel Kvalvik, faithful member of
the *I Serve* team at VLife Church,
McKinney, Texas

DEDICATION

I am dedicating my book, <u>Holy Ghost Primer</u>, to Mark McKay. Back in the early 80's I was a staff pastor at a church in Seattle, and Mark was my pastor. At that point in my ministry career, I had been a staff pastor at six different churches in Washington and California, and I had also started a new church as founding pastor. So I was gaining experience in the ministry, as well as developing deeper understanding of the Bible. I had a reputation as a student of the Word, and I was proud of it. I considered myself more of a Berean than a charismatic because I always searched the Word diligently on any and every topic.

One evening Pastor McKay and I traveled to one of our sister churches for a special service. They were ordaining men as leaders in their church, and we were to be there as part of the presbytery. We would lay hands on the men, pray, set them in place and prophesy. As the ordination proceeded, there were several personal prophecies spoken over the men. It was a tremendous spiritual experience, but I was not paying much attention to the actual words of the personal prophecies. Then an unusual thing happened. One man (I don't remember who he was) spoke a personal prophecy over one of the men being ordained as a deacon. When he finished, Mark McKay calmly asked for the microphone, and proceeded to correct something that had been said in the personal prophecy. He didn't yell, he didn't rebuke, he didn't shame; he just clearly corrected what had been said and made sure that the new deacon understood. My head was in a whirl: once Mark spoke, the error was obvious, but I hadn't caught it. In fact it was almost like I didn't know what was going on. Men of God were speaking things that they said were from the Holy Spirit, and I was just praying and going along with whatever. Mark's words of correction were well received by everyone present, and the service went on to an appropriate ending.

As Mark and I were driving back to West Seattle (he was driving), I asked him, "How did you know that the prophecy was wrong?" His answer was simple and direct: "I listen carefully with my mind, and I depend upon the Holy Spirit to tell me what's right and wrong." He went on to tell me that when you are in a leadership position of authority, you have to be on guard and to have the faith for the Holy Spirit to tell you what's going on. I have not had any communication with Mark since the late 80's, but his input was of great value to my walk with the Holy Spirit.

That was the time I came to realize that I had not been "aware" like a leader should be aware. I vowed before the Lord that I would never again just pray and go along with whatever. God expected me to be a "spiritually aware" leader and to speak and act accordingly, just as the Holy Spirit expected me to. From that time I have been faithful to pay attention to what is being said, and especially pay attention to the voice of the Holy Spirit, confirming, correcting or checking. The Holy Spirit has never failed me in that. I have become secure and comfortable in my relationship with the Holy Spirit. My father in the Lord, Dick Benjamin, has said that I am a man who is comfortable in my relationship with the Holy Spirit. I like that statement, and agree with it. But I mark that night with Mark as the time that my relationship with the Holy Spirit changed from "being in awe, and praying, but not really paying attention," to "carefully listening and closely being aware of the presence and voice of the Holy Spirit." And it has worked! I am comfortable with my relationship with the Holy Spirit. Thank you, Mark, for your input. It has been of great value to my ministry and to the kingdom of the Lord Jesus Christ.

CONTENTS

Preface: Why the Rise Above Series?...................11

Introduction..15

Part One: Baptism with the Holy Spirit - For Power

Chapter One	Baptism with the Holy Spirit......25	
	He will baptize you with the	
	Holy Spirit and fire	
Chapter Two	With You or In You?....................33	
	At what moment does the Holy Spirit	
	reside in a Christian?	
Chapter Three	What are We Waiting On?..........43	
	Tarry ye until you be endued	
	with power	
Chapter Four	The Day of Pentecost..................51	
	Speaking and Utterance:	
	Who does what?	
Chapter Five	The House of Cornelius...............59	
	While Peter was still speaking,	
	the Holy Spirit fell	
Chapter Six	Disciples in Ephesus....................67	
	Did you receive the Holy Spirit	
	when you believed?	
Chapter Seven	My Baptism with the	
	Holy Spirit...................................73	
	The deal I made with God	

Part Two: Speaking in Tongues - For Edification

Chapter Eight	It's Good for You!..........83 *Not to be feared, fought or forbidden*	
Chapter Nine	Seven Gems from I Corinthians 14..........93 *Instruction for the Charismatic Corinthian Congregation*	
Chapter Ten	Praying in the Spirit..........103 *A key gift that the Holy Spirit uses to build us up*	
Chapter Eleven	Is This Gift for You?..........111 *It was good for Paul, but is it good enough for you?*	

Part Three: Gifts of the Spirit - For Touching God's People

Chapter Twelve	Holy Spirit Ministry Gifts..........117 *Regular people touching regular people with God's special help*	
Chapter Thirteen	Word of Wisdom and Word of Knowledge..........129 *Regular people speaking divine revelations of wisdom and knowledge to regular people*	
Chapter Fourteen	Gifts of Healing..........139 *God supernaturally healing people through regular people*	
Chapter Fifteen	Prophecy..........151 *God speaking revelations to build up, warn and comfort His people*	
Chapter Sixteen	Distinguishing of Spirits..........161 *God helping His people to know spirits and act accordingly*	

Chapter Seventeen	Final Principles of Practice for the Gifts..................................167
	Regular people successfully exercising Holy Spirit ministry gifts

In Closing..175

Preface

WHY THE RISE ABOVE SERIES?

Isaiah 2:2, 3 – The word which Isaiah the son of Amoz saw concerning Judah and Jerusalem. Now it will come about that in the last days the mountain of the house of the LORD will be established as the chief of the mountains, and will be raised above the hills; and all the nations will stream to it. And many peoples will come and say, "Come let us go up to the mountain of the LORD, to the house of the God of Jacob; that He may teach us concerning His ways and that we may walk in His paths." For the law will go forth from Zion and the word of the LORD from Jerusalem.

Micah 1:1; 4:1, 2 – The word of the LORD which came to Micah of Moresheth…And it will come about in the last days that the mountain of the house of the LORD will be established as the chief of the mountains. It will be raised above the hills, and the peoples will stream to it. Many nations will come and say, "Come and let us go up to the mountain of the LORD and to the house of the God of Jacob, that He may teach us about His ways and that we may walk in His paths." For from Zion will go forth the law, even the word of the LORD from Jerusalem.

Matthew 5:14-16 – You are the light of the world. A city set on a hill cannot be hidden; nor does anyone light a lamp and put it under a basket, but on the lampstand, and it gives light to all who are in the house. Let your light shine before men in such a way that they may see your good works, and glorify your Father who is in heaven.

Matthew 28:19, 20 – Go therefore and make disciples of all the nations, baptizing them in the name of the Father and the Son and the Holy Spirit, teaching them to observe all that I commanded you; and lo, I am with you always, even to the end of the age.

John 10:10 – The thief comes only to steal and kill and destroy; I came that they may have life, and have it abundantly.

All of these Scriptures are talking about the church of the Lord Jesus Christ in the last days, describing how people from all nations and people groups will come into the church. It is all about the end times ingathering of people into the kingdom of God and into the church of our Lord.

Back in the eighth century B.C., during the reigns of the Kings Ahaz and Hezekiah in the nation of Judah, we had two very different scenarios of what happened to the house of God (the Jerusalem temple). It can be summed up very simply: King Ahaz closed the doors of the house of the LORD (II Chronicles 28:24); King Hezekiah opened the doors of the house of the LORD (II Chronicles 29:3). There were also two prophets (Isaiah and Micah) who spoke identical prophecies about the very last days. Isaiah came from an aristocratic family, while Micah was a peasant farmer: two very different classes, but an identical prophecy from the LORD. This end time prophecy, through shadow and substance, tells the end times church exactly how people will be attracted to and come into the church of the Lord Jesus Christ.

The mountain of the house of the LORD, the mountain of the LORD, the house of the God of Jacob, Zion and Jerusalem are all terms referring to the temple in Jerusalem, where God's presence resided. In the New Testament, the church is the

PREFACE: WHY THE RISE ABOVE SERIES?

temple of God, for His presence resides inside every person who has accepted Jesus Christ as Savior and Lord. This is what the Old Testament prophecy is saying to the church:

- In the last days the church of the Lord Jesus Christ will be raised above all other religions, philosophies and movements. As it is established as chief among all religions, many people from all nations and all kinds of people groups will come into the church, looking to learn the ways of the LORD and how to walk in His paths. Simply put, there will be a large group of people who will become Christians.

This is what I referred to earlier as the end times ingathering. We want this to happen, and it is clearly the will of God, for He is not willing for any to perish, but for all to come to repentance (II Peter 3:9). So how will the church rise above the hills, that is, the religions, philosophies and movements of the world? The answer is found in the teachings of Jesus during the Sermon on the Mount. The church becomes like a city set on a hill: it can't be hidden. The people in the church will be a light that shines out to all people. We are to shine in such a way that they see our good works and glorify God. Our good works are our very lives: our abundant lives. People will see the abundant lives that we live in Jesus, and come into the church to learn more; they will marvel at the ways of the LORD that give us abundant life, and accepting Christ, they will walk in the same abundant lives that we show them.

We have used many methods to shine forth our light and spread the gospel (T.V., internet, social media, evangelism crusades, door-to-door witnessing, tracts, street preaching, picketing, political involvement, etc.) and we spend millions of dollars on those methods. But are we seeing the end times ingathering, with masses of people coming into the church?

Certainly not in the United States. So I ask another question: are we living the abundant life in Jesus Christ that shows itself as far superior to other religions, philosophies and life styles? Are the people of the world looking at the people in the church and saying, "Wow! Their lives are far superior to and way above anything we are seeing or experiencing. Let's go into the church of Jesus Christ and check it out!" The answer is no. On a one-to-one scale, there are some individuals who come into the church for this very reason, but not on the massive scale spoken of in the prophecies of Isaiah and Micah.

We, the church of Jesus Christ, need to focus our attention on living the successful, powerful, abundant life that God has for us. In every aspect of life: marriage, child-raising, work, business, finances, physical health, mental health, spiritual dimension, etc., we need to live our lives in such a way that it shines brightly and brings people into the church to check it out. Instead of settling for a so-so or struggling life, and making it to heaven by the skin of our teeth, we need to live the abundant life that results in many coming into the church. So the books of the "Rise Above" series are all about Christians learning to walk in the abundant life. Rise above, and see the harvest of people coming into the church to learn the ways of the Lord and how to walk in them. Many people will come to Jesus Christ to have the abundant life!

<u>Holy Ghost Primer</u> is a book about every Christian shedding inhibitions and hesitations about the Holy Spirit, and using every baptism, gift and fruit of the Spirit to live the accelerated, abundant Christian life. Enjoy it, learn and increase your abundant life. Rise above!

INTRODUCTION

In the twenty-first century it sometimes appears that the successful churches, pastors and Christians are a bit hesitant and standoffish when it comes to teachings about the Holy Spirit. In the 20th century, during the many years of the Pentecostal Movement and the charismatic movement, a lot of things were taught, practiced and institutionalized regarding the things of the Spirit: some good things, some bad things, some things that built the church of Jesus Christ, and some things that hurt Christians. It seemed, at times, that Pentecostals and charismatics could not conduct themselves decently and in order. Because of these errors in teaching and practice, Christian leaders began backing away from the things of the Spirit. It sometimes seems that it is better to just avoid these Holy Spirit areas, because they can be too emotional and lead to errors and mistakes. Some present-day leaders take an open stand against Christians who practice speaking in tongues or prophesying, while other leaders just avoid the topics. It is true that we need to avoid offending people or turning them off, but avoiding the topics is not the answer. It is possible to live and walk in the fullness of the Holy Spirit, and do it in such a way that it is decent and orderly, and builds up everyone. As our mothers taught us from an early age: don't throw out the baby with the bath water.

I am a Pentecostal. I was raised in Pentecostal churches from a young age, and I experienced the teachings and the practices of those denominations. Pentecostals placed a strong emphasis on the Day of Pentecost experience recorded in Acts chapter two: people being baptized in the Holy Spirit and speaking in tongues as evidence. They also strongly emphasized the gifts of the Holy Spirit; especially the gift of tongues and interpretation of tongues. I heard good and bad doctrine; I saw good and bad examples of the gifts of the Spirit being exercised. I want to live my Christian life in the fullness of the Spirit, following the good teachings and practices of the Pentecostals, while avoiding the errors and mistakes.

I am a charismatic. I ministered in charismatic churches for over twenty years, and I experienced the teachings and the practices of several non-denominational, fundamental, charismatic, Bible-believing congregations. Charismatics placed a strong emphasis on the "charisma," that is, the gifts of the Holy Spirit, especially prophecy, the word of wisdom and the word of knowledge. I heard good and bad teachings; I saw good and bad examples of the gifts of the Spirit being exercised. I want to live my Christian life in the fullness of the Spirit, following the good teachings and practices of the charismatics, while avoiding the errors and mistakes.

Maybe you are a Pentecostal; maybe you're not. Maybe you are a charismatic; maybe you're not. But you and I are both Christians, because we have accepted Jesus Christ as our Savior and Lord. And as Christians, you and I both have the Holy Spirit inside of us, so we both want to have everything God has for us in His Holy Spirit. In this book I want to teach the close and powerful communion we are to have with the Holy Spirit. I want to approach this in a simple and straightforward way. I want every one of us to have everything God wants us to have. I don't want bad teachings or bad practices

INTRODUCTION

that we have seen or heard about to hold us back from our unity and community with God's Spirit. Walk with me as we work through the Scriptures to become informed participants in God's "Holy Spirit plans." After all, it is much better to pursue knowledge and truth, than to practice avoidance because of other people's choices or mistakes.

Holy Smoke…Holy Fire…Holy Ghost. These are terms that people have used when they were referring to mighty things that have occurred in the church over the last many years: things that God has done supernaturally by His Spirit.

Holy smoke is a reference to the Old Testament practice of burning the sacrifices to God. When the fat began to burn, smoke would rise up as an aroma, acceptable and pleasing to God. In the New Testament fulfillment of the Old Testament type, when Jesus died on the cross for our sins, His sacrifice was the ultimate fragrant smoke and aroma to God.

Ephesians 5:2 – just as Christ also loved you and gave Himself up for us, an offering and a sacrifice to God as a fragrant aroma.

You will sometimes hear the old timers refer to some special revival meeting, or healing service, in which people could feel the presence of the Lord, and experienced an overall powerful, God-filled atmosphere. They might say, "It was like holy smoke filled the room." They use the phrase in a positive way to designate a special experience of God's presence.

Holy fire may refer to different events in the Bible, some positive and some negative. When God revealed Himself to Moses in the wilderness it was initially through a burning bush. Moses saw this bush that was burning with fire, but was not consumed. When he turned aside to take a closer look, God began to speak to Him. When the Israelites went out in mass from their bondage in Egypt, God's presence with them was manifested by a pillar cloud during the day. When night came the pillar cloud became a pillar of fire. That manifestation stayed with the Israelites for 40 years, as they wandered the wilderness. When Elijah challenged the prophets of Baal to a contest, the challenge was which god would send fire from heaven to consume the sacrifice. When the LORD God sent the fire, then the people rose up against the prophets of Baal and killed them. When Solomon offered the sacrifice to dedicate the temple, God sent fire from heaven, and the temple was filled with the smoke, glory and presence of God. Thus holy fire often signaled the presence and approval of God. There were also times that fire represented God's disapproval. When Nadab and Abihu brought fire to the altar of the Lord, without doing it correctly, fire shot out from the altar and consumed them in judgment. Many times fire is referred to as the instrument of judgment upon disobedience and wickedness. Fire has been associated with the Holy Spirit in our time because of two particular New Testament references. One is a statement from John the Baptist about the coming Messiah:

*Luke 3:16,17 – John answered and said to them all, "As for me, I baptize you with water, but One is coming who is mightier than I, and I am not fit to untie the thong of His sandals; He will baptize you with the Holy Spirit and **fire**. His winnowing fork is in His hand to thoroughly clear his threshing floor, and to gather the wheat into His barn; but He will burn up the chaff with unquenchable fire."*

The other is the day of Pentecost when the believers were filled with the Holy Spirit.

Acts 1:4 – Gathering them together, He commanded them not to leave Jerusalem, but to wait for what the Father had promised, "Which," He said, "you heard of from Me; for John baptized with water, but you will be baptized with the Holy Spirit not many days from now."

INTRODUCTION

*Acts 2:3 – And there appeared to them **tongues as of fire** distributing themselves, and they rested on each one of them. And they were all filled with the Holy Spirit and began to speak with other tongues, as the Spirit was giving them utterance.*

Jesus made it clear that the disciples were to wait in Jerusalem until they received power from on high. As He had told them before, John baptized with water, but they would be baptized with the Holy Spirit in just a few days. I don't know what tongues of fire resting on each one of them looked like. Whatever it was, it could be seen, it didn't harm them and it was part of the very positive experience of being filled with the Holy Spirit! That sounds like positive holy fire to me. With regard to John the Baptist declaring that the Messiah would baptize them with the Holy Spirit and fire, we can see that being baptized with the Holy Spirit was positive. But being baptized with fire might not be connected with Holy Spirit baptism, but instead with the destruction of chaff by fire. That is certainly what the very next verse states. While some Christians have referred to being baptized with fire as a powerful, necessary experience for Christians to have, I will discuss this more in the pages to come, showing that all Christians should want and seek the baptism with the Holy Spirit, but no Christian should want or go through the baptism of fire.

Holy Ghost. Back in the day of King James I of England, and the English translation of the Bible that he authorized, they used the phrase "Holy Ghost" to refer to the third person of the Godhead. During the first half of the twentieth century, as the Pentecostal movement swept through the Midwest, up the west coast, and then all over the continent, Christians were re-vitalized in their relationship with God and their involvement in the work of the ministry. As a child in the 50's

I can still remember different pastors and teachers who would shout out things like:

> "The Holy Ghost is in the house today!"
> "We are standing on holy ground;
> this is Holy Ghost ground!"
> "You need the Holy Ghost!"
> "Did you receive the Holy Ghost when you believed?"
> "Are you baptized in the Holy Ghost?"

Even today my pastor refers to the Holy Ghost at times, to bring attention to the Holy Spirit, the third person of the Godhead. When the organizers of a "haunted tour" for our local town were talking with Pastor Mike, they asked him whether our old church building was haunted: did we have any ghosts? He responded, "Oh yes, every time we get together here at the church there is a very powerful ghost present. People can feel him; they believe in him, they even think he speaks through some of them!" Saying things like that can get "haunted tour" people pretty excited.

It's almost like we see the Holy Spirit as "one-third of God."

The Holy Ghost is the Holy Spirit. Every Christian should have their most intimate and divine relationship with Him. He is the third person of the Godhead. But in our attempts to understand our one God, eternally existent in three persons: God the Father, God the Son and God the Holy Spirit, we somehow truncate the Godhead. It's almost like we see the Holy Spirit as "one-third of God." We relate to the Father for some things, Jesus Christ for some things and the Holy Spirit

INTRODUCTION

for some things. It's almost like we treat the Holy Spirit as the lesser part of God. What we need to accept is that the fullness of the Godhead dwells in Jesus Christ in bodily form. The fullness of the Godhead is in the Father; the fullness of the Godhead is in the Son; the fullness of the Godhead is in the Holy Spirit. I didn't say we need to understand it; I said we need to accept it. Every time I speak to the Father, I am addressing the fullness of God; every time I speak to Jesus, I am addressing the fullness of God; every time I ask the Holy Spirit to help me, I am asking the fullness of God to help me. The LORD our God is one God, regardless of how we address him, or which title we use to speak to Him. Every Christian has the Holy Spirit inside of them: that means God is inside of you and me. If you are a Christian, you got a ghost in you: God!

If you are not sure that you are a Christian, or that the Spirit of God is within you, I want you to gain the fullest possible benefit from this Holy Ghost primer. Going to church does not make us Christians. Hanging around Christians does not make us Christians. Performing religious acts does not make us Christians. Only by accepting the free gift of eternal life from Jesus Christ and inviting Him to come into our hearts and lives can we be saved and partake of the relationship and inner dwelling that He has given us in the Holy Spirit.

If you have done this, you have the necessary communion with His Spirit to partake of these truths about baptism, ministry gifts and guidance. If you have not, I invite you now to become a Christian. Pray this prayer right now, and you will be born again and begin establishing your personal relationship with Jesus Christ.

"Dear Jesus, thank you for dying on the Cross for me. Please forgive my sins and come into my heart and life. I step down from the throne of my heart, and ask you to sit there. I will abide in You, as you abide in Me. Help me walk in unity with You and with my fellow Christians, so that I can live the abundant life you want me to live. I accept that I am saved by faith and grace. I love you Lord. Amen."

Now moving forward as Christians, with the Spirit of God within us, let's look sincerely at baptism with the Holy Spirit for power, speaking in tongues for edification, the gifts of the Spirit for touching God's people, and how to responsibly minister God's special gifts. Our very own Holy Ghost primer!

Part One

Baptism with the Holy Spirit – For Power

"He will baptize you with the Holy Spirit and fire"

Luke 3:16

Chapter One

BAPTISM WITH THE HOLY SPIRIT

He will baptize you with the Holy Spirit and fire

Baptism with the Holy Spirit is an expectation and experience taught by the Bible. It involves all of the Godhead; it is promised to believers by the Father, it is an action taken by Jesus, that John the Baptist predicted concerning the expected coming Messiah (Christ, the Anointed One), and it is accomplished by the Holy Spirit in the life and heart of every Christian believer.

The early church believed it to be part and parcel of becoming a Christian and, on more than one occasion, apostles were called upon to make sure that new believers received this gift of the Holy Spirit. It was referred to by different phrases: baptized with the Holy Spirit, filled with the Holy Spirit, receiving the Holy Spirit, the Holy Spirit falling on someone, the Holy Spirit coming on someone, etc. The variety of phrases used to refer to this same event or happening, allows us to relax somewhat about the exact language to be used. Both John the Baptist and Jesus referred to this experience as baptism with the Holy Spirit, so I will use that phrase throughout this teaching.

> **The purpose of being baptized with the Holy Spirit is to receive power.**

The purpose of being baptized with the Holy Spirit is to receive power, and that power is to be used to spread the gospel of Jesus Christ, to accomplish whatever work of the ministry that Jesus Christ wants each of us to be doing. Our hearts, as Christians, must be set on seeking His kingdom and His righteousness. We should be using every tool, teaching and experience that we can to accomplish His will. In these times God has promised that He will bring all kinds of nations and people groups into the church, and He expects the church to respond to all of them by teaching them the ways of the Lord and how they can walk in them. That's what they will be looking for when they come in, and that's what we need to teach them; no more and certainly no less! The release of power that the baptism with the Holy Spirit can bring to each of us is necessary and crucial to the fulfillment of our mission and commission. The baptism with the Holy Spirit releases the power that is within each of us. With that power we can attain all of the abundant life and ministry that He desires for us.

Please understand that I am a Pentecostal and I share that information with pride. My parents attended Pentecostal churches, and brought the kids to church (even when we didn't want to go). I remember Foursquare churches, Assemblies of God churches, independent Pentecostal churches; I even remember one called the Church of God of

BAPTISM WITH THE HOLY SPIRIT

Prophecy! (I have two childhood memories of that church: the ladies of that church knew how to make pulled taffy – it was delicious; and I also remember thinking the preacher was going to break through the platform floor – he stomped so hard when he preached!)

The Pentecostals of my experience placed a strong emphasis on the Day of Pentecost event recorded in Acts chapter two: people being baptized in the Holy Spirit and speaking in tongues as evidence. They also strongly emphasized the gifts of the Holy Spirit; especially the gift of tongues and interpretation of tongues. I sat under the teachings of the second generation from the early twentieth century revivals, such as Azusa Street in California. There were real, genuine, Biblical teachings and experiences shared by these people. I am thankful to the Pentecostal leaders that gave me solid teaching and guidance.

There were also excesses, errors and mistakes. When you combine experiences, humans and emotions, you have the potential for mistakes, errors and incorrect teaching. I have seen and experienced that in my Pentecostal circles. The reason I am still a Pentecostal and take pride in it is because of the real, genuine, Biblical teachings and experiences that I was privileged to be a part of. Baptism with the Holy Spirit as expressed in Acts chapter 2 is real. And the gifts of the Holy Spirit as expressed in I Corinthians chapters 12, 13 and 14 are real.

Also please understand that I am a charismatic and I share that information with pride. I was part of several different charismatic churches in the 70's and 80's, and gained fresh perspective on the things of the Spirit. I remember being an advisor to Women's Aglow, regularly attending Full Gospel Businessmen's Fellowship International, attending Catholic afterglow meetings, meeting with Jesus People, and gaining a whole new perspective on the things of the Spirit, from a perspective outside of Pentecostal circles.

The charismatics of my experience placed a strong emphasis on the "charisma," that is, the gifts of the Holy Spirit enumerated in I Corinthians chapter 12, especially the gifts of prophecy, word of wisdom and word of knowledge. Uniquely, both leaders and followers in the charismatic movement saw themselves as trans-denominational and not tied to any one local church. I sat under the teachings of Episcopalian and Catholic leaders, as well as non-denominational leaders, such as the Florida Five. There were real, genuine Biblical teachings and experiences shared by these people. I am proud to be called a charismatic and I am thankful for the teachings that pointed me in the direction of Holy Spirit power and non-sectarian fellowship.

There were also excesses, errors and mistakes. As I have said before, when you combine experiences, humans and emotions, you have the potential for mistakes, errors and incorrect teaching. I have seen and experienced that in my charismatic circles. The reason I still call myself a charismatic and take pride in it is because of the real, genuine, Biblical teachings and experiences that I was privileged to be a part of. Baptism with the Holy Spirit as expressed in Acts chapter 2 is real. And the gifts of the Holy Spirit as expressed in I Corinthians chapters 12, 13 and 14 are real. So let's consider the relevant New Testament Scriptures.

Luke 3:16, 17 – John answered and said to them all, "As for me, I baptize you with water; but One is coming who is mightier than I, and I am not fit to untie the thong of His sandals; **He will baptize you with the Holy Spirit and fire.** *His winnowing fork is in His hand to* *thoroughly clear His threshing floor, and to gather the wheat into His barn; but He will burn up the chaff with unquenchable fire."*

John preached a baptism of repentance for the forgiveness of sins. There were crowds of people coming out to hear him, and to be baptized. He did not mince words: "You brood of vipers, who warned you to flee from the wrath to come?" He made it clear that if they didn't repent and change, they were about to be destroyed in words similar to this: "the axe is already laid at the root of the tree. You're about to be cut down and thrown into the fire." All kinds of people came and asked what they should do, including tax collectors and soldiers (undoubtedly mentioned because they were the most despised by the Jewish people). And he would give them very specific answers. At that time people were in a state of expectation, sensing that God was about to move. Could it be that John might be the promised Messiah; the Christ? They must have asked him, because that is what prompted his response. "I baptize you with water;…He will baptize you with the Holy Spirit and fire."

Baptism with fire is a very bad thing.

Baptism with fire! I want to address the second part of John's statement, about Jesus baptizing with fire. I have heard some people say that this is just another way of referring to baptism with the Holy Spirit. They point to the day of Pentecost, in which tongues as of fire distributed themselves and rested on each one of them. Surely this is a fulfillment of the prophetic statement of John the Baptist. This interpretation is interesting, and on the face of it, seems harmless. Once we examine the contextual meaning we must conclude that baptism with fire as mentioned by John is something that a Christian never wants to experience. Baptism with fire is a very bad thing.

Other people over the years have put a far more separate and unique interpretation on this baptism of fire. They see it as a special experience that happens after you become a Christian, and after you have been baptized with the Holy Spirit. They believe that in the course of your walk and ministry in the Lord, there comes a time when God must finally break you and break your will in such a way that you are finally totally broken down and surrendering to His will. It is from this point that you move forward in power, with signs and wonders manifest, doing the greater works that God intended that you do for Him and for His kingdom. The people who believe in this idea of baptism of fire believe it so strongly that they almost develop it into a Trinity Experience doctrine: the first biggy is salvation, the second biggy is baptism with the Holy Spirit and the third biggy is baptism with fire. If you have run into someone who has had this "experience" you'll understand when I say that they tend to be obsessed with this experience, and possessed with the desire to somehow feel that same experience of baptism with fire again and again. The ones I have met who proclaim this baptism with fire tend to be long on experiential emotions and short on real power and accomplishments for God's kingdom. It's funny how God's people can camp out on some special experience in their life, but not move forward into what God really wants them to accomplish in the work of the ministry.

The Bible does teach that we can have special experiences with the Spirit of God that are subsequent to our salvation time and our time of getting baptized with the Holy Spirit. For example:

BAPTISM WITH THE HOLY SPIRIT

Acts 4:31 – And when they had prayed, the place where they had gathered together was shaken, and they were all filled with the Holy Spirit and began to speak the word of God with boldness.

Peter and John had been used by God to bring healing to the lame man at the Beautiful Gate of the temple. Peter preached an amazing gospel message and five thousand more people became Christians. They had then been arrested, jailed overnight, hauled before the Jewish religious authorities the next day and rebuked for preaching the gospel of Jesus Christ. They were threatened and then released. They got together with their companions and gave them a report of everything that had happened. And then they prayed: "Lord, take note of their threats, and grant that Your bondservants may speak Your word with all confidence, while You extend Your hand to heal, and signs and wonders take place through the name of Your holy servant Jesus." God immediately answered their prayer, shaking the place where they were gathered and filling them with the Holy Spirit. They went forth speaking the word of God with boldness. And signs and wonders did follow them as they preached! Peter and John and their companions who experienced this were part of the group of believers that were filled with the Holy Spirit, as recorded back in Acts 2:4, on the day of Pentecost. This is a clear example of being "filled with the Holy Spirit" as an experience subsequent to being baptized in the Holy Spirit. As you follow the Christian leaders and believers through the book of Acts, you can find many specific, special events in which a believer or group of believers are "filled" with the Spirit, subsequent to being baptized with the Holy Spirit.

When a person accepts Jesus Christ as Savior and Lord, the Holy Spirit takes up residence in him. As a Christian, God is inside of him, all the time. At times a Christian is not aware of God's presence in them, but He is still there. There are other special times that a Christian becomes very aware of, and in tune with the Holy Spirit within him. I believe that the more we are in tune with the Holy Spirit, the more He can freely and powerfully move in us and through us. That's what the Bible refers to as being filled with the Spirit.

But back to the concept of being baptized with fire. When John the Baptist spoke about Jesus Christ baptizing people with the Holy Spirit and with fire, he was not speaking about two positive things. A careful examination of the immediate context and John's ministry show that John's message was a call to repentance, and that God was separating the wheat from the chaff. God will winnow and thresh His people. The ones that are wheat (that's positive) are baptized with the Holy Spirit and are gathered into His barn. The ones that are chaff are baptized with fire; burned with unquenchable fire. Those that repent and receive Him receive baptism with the Holy Spirit; those that do not repent and receive Him receive baptism with fire. You and I, as Christians, do not want to experience the baptism of fire that John the Baptist proclaimed. And so, declare with me unto the Lord:

"I am wheat and I choose You; baptize me with Your Holy Spirit. I am not chaff that has rejected You, and You will not have to baptize me with fire. I choose to be baptized, not burned!"

Chapter Two

WITH YOU OR IN YOU?

At what moment does the Holy Spirit reside in a Christian?

John 14:16,17 – I will ask the Father, and He will give you another Helper, that He may be with you forever; that is the Spirit of truth, whom the world cannot receive, because it does not see Him or know Him, but you know Him because He abides **with you** *and* **will be in you.**

On the final night before He was to be arrested, tried and crucified, Jesus covered many important teachings with His disciples. (I have covered those teachings in another book entitled: The Final Night). In these verses He was imparting to them instructions on how to continue intimate relationship with Him in and through the Holy Spirit.

Disciples of Christ (including us) often don't pay attention to what He is telling them.

There is a unique Greek term used here to refer to the Holy Spirit: the Paraclete. The word has been variously translated as Helper, Counselor, Comforter, Advocate, etc. It refers to one who is called alongside you to help, like a defense attorney/legal advisor in court. It's like having a companion with you all the time that gives you the best and correct advice about anything and everything. Don't miss the fact that He is called "another" Helper. Jesus Himself had been physically present with His disciples for 3½ years, and during that time He had been the Helper for them. On that final night it was obvious to Him that they were still very dependent upon His physical presence and counsel. He did His best to inform them and to prepare them for His death and departure, but as you know, disciples of Christ (including us) often don't pay attention to what He is telling them. He knew things were about to change for them, and so He promised that Father God would provide the Holy Spirit to be their ever present Helper. The great thing is that the Holy Spirit as their Helper was going to be with them far longer than 3½ years: He would be with them forever!

He also referred to the Holy Spirit as the Spirit of truth. As God, the Holy Spirit knows everything. He is eternal, and knows all truth, past, present and future. Jesus said of Himself, "I am the way and the truth and the life." So too, the Holy Spirit is the truth: our Spirit of Truth. This was an extraordinary title that Jesus used, and on that final night He provided a broad palette of actions that the Spirit of truth would perform for His disciples: He would teach them all things; He would bring to their remembrance all that Jesus had ever said to them; He would guide them into all the truth; He would disclose to them what was to come; He would disclose the things of the Father and the Son to them. All of these actions are phenomenal and the beauty is that while the world could not even receive the Spirit of truth because of their unbelief, the disciples already knew Him. Now how could Jesus say that? The answer is simple, once you see it:

the Spirit of Truth abided with them. What? Who had abided with them for 3½ years? Jesus Himself! Jesus Himself is one and the same as the Holy Spirit, the Spirit of Truth. Scripture says very clearly that the Lord is the Spirit (II Corinthians 3:17). Scripture also says that all the fullness of the Godhead dwells in Jesus Christ in bodily form (Colossians 2:9).

II Corinthians 3:17 – Now the Lord is the Spirit, and where the Spirit of the Lord is, there is liberty.

Colossians 2:9 – For in Him all the fullness of Deity dwells in bodily form,...

The Comforter and Spirit of Truth that Jesus was promising to His disciples was Himself, but in His spiritual dimension (spirit) form. The Holy Spirit isn't somebody different; He is Jesus. He was with them physically for the 3½ years of His public ministry; after His death on the cross and their immediate salvation by belief in Him, He would be in them as the Holy Spirit. That's the beauty of the New Covenant: God now dwells within each Christian believer!

He abides with you and will be in you. That statement about the Holy Spirit has been misinterpreted by some Pentecostals to mean that when a person becomes a Christian the Holy Spirit is with them. Then at a subsequent event, namely their baptism with the Holy Spirit, He would be in them: with them at salvation, then in them at their baptism with the Holy Spirit. They point to the time separation (about 50 days) between the Crucifixion and the Day of Pentecost when the Holy Spirit filled the disciples. They say that the salvation of the disciples was accomplished at the moment of the death of Christ on the cross, but the Holy Spirit was not technically in them until the Day of Pentecost when they were all filled with the Holy Spirit. The Holy Spirit was with them at salvation, but not in them until they were baptized with the Holy Spirit about 50 days later. With them at salvation…in them at baptism with the Holy Spirit. But this is not true, because Scripture teaches us again and again that the Holy Spirit is inside every Christian, and a person becomes a Christian at the moment they accept Jesus Christ as Savior and Lord. Read the following verses:

Romans 8:9-11 – However, you are not in the flesh but in the Spirit, if indeed the Spirit of God dwells in you. But if anyone does not have the Spirit of Christ, he does not belong to Him. If Christ is in you, though the body is dead because of sin, yet the spirit is alive because of righteousness. But if the Spirit of Him who raised Jesus from the dead dwells in you, He who raised Christ Jesus from the dead will also give life to your mortal bodies through His Spirit who dwells in you.

I Corinthians 3:16 – Do you not know that you are a temple of God and that the Spirit of God dwells in you?

I Corinthians 6:19 – Or do you not know that your body is a temple of the Holy Spirit who is in you, whom you have from God, and that you are not your own?

Galatians 3:2, 3 – This is the only thing I want to find out from you: did you receive the Spirit by the works of the Law, or by hearing with faith?

Why did God wait until the Day of Pentecost for His disciples to be filled with the Holy Spirit and receive power? When Jesus died on the cross, paying the penalty for the sins of mankind, the disciples were saved and the Spirit of God took up residence in each of them. So why the delay before the special release of Holy Spirit power? The answer is one that we don't think a lot about. The feasts and holidays of the Jewish calendar were types and shadows of the truths of the New Covenant. Jesus was crucified at Passover, and that special feast commemorated when the death angel passed over Egypt, saw the blood of the lamb on the door posts and beams of the homes of the Israelites, and spared them from death. That is prophetic (shadow and substance) of the shed blood of Jesus on the cross rescuing us from the sentence of death for our sins. So too the day of Pentecost was a special feast day with special type and shadow truths in the New Covenant.

Leviticus 23:15-22 – You shall also count for yourselves from the day after the Sabbath, from the day when you brought in the sheaf of the wave offering; there shall be seven complete Sabbaths. You shall count fifty days to the day after the seventh sabbath; then you shall present a new grain offering to the LORD. You shall bring in from your dwelling places two loaves of bread for a wave offering, made of two-tenths of an ephah; they shall be of a fine flour, baked with leaven as first fruits to the LORD. Along with the bread you shall present seven one year old male lambs without defect, and a bull of the herd and two rams; they are to be a burnt offering to the LORD, with their grain offering and their drink offerings, an offering by fire of a soothing aroma to the LORD. You shall also offer one male goat for a sin offering and two male lambs one year old for a sacrifice of peace offerings. The priest shall then wave them with the bread of the first fruits for a wave offering with two lambs before the LORD; they are to be holy to the LORD for the priest. **On this same day you shall make a proclamation as well; you are to have a holy convocation.** *You shall do no laborious work. It is to be a perpetual statute in all your dwelling places throughout your generations. When you reap the harvest of your land, moreover, you shall not reap to the very* **corners of your field** *nor gather the* **gleaning of your harvest***; you are to leave them for the needy and the alien. I am the LORD your God.*

Deuteronomy 16:9-11 – You shall count seven weeks for yourself; you shall begin to count seven weeks from the time you begin to put the sickle to the standing grain. Then you shall celebrate the **Feast of Weeks** *to the LORD your God with a tribute of a freewill offering of your hand, which you shall give just as the LORD your God blesses you; and you shall rejoice before the LORD your God, you and your son* *and your daughter and your male and female servants and the Levite who is in your town, and the stranger and the orphan and the widow who are in your midst, in the place where the LORD your God chooses to establish His name.*

There were three Feasts each year that were very special to the Israelites: Passover, Weeks and Tabernacles.

(See also Exodus 23:16 and 34:22). Pentecost was another name for the Feast of Weeks, or the Feast of the Harvest of the first fruits. It was a one-day feast that occurred fifty days after the Passover Feast (50 = Pentecost). There were three Feasts each year that were very special to the Israelites: Passover, Weeks and Tabernacles. On these three Feast occasions all male Israelites had to make a pilgrimage to the center of worship. In the first century that would have been the temple in Jerusalem. The Feast of Weeks was an agricultural festival that marked the beginning of the wheat harvest. The first fruits of the wheat harvest were offered as a special wave offering. Also two loaves of leavened bread, called the bread of the first fruits, made from fine flour, were presented to the Lord as a meal offering, for use in the tabernacle/temple. It signified that even our daily bread was provided by God. It was to be a joyous celebration for everyone participating. At the Holy Convocation (the assembly or gathering), special proclamation was to be made about the whole first fruits participation. That proclamation included a careful reminder that in the midst of the joyous celebration, they were not to forget the less fortunate; even the poor and needy were to be provided for by not reaping the corners of the wheat fields,

WITH YOU OR IN YOU?

and not gathering up the loose/leftover grain in the field (called the gleanings). That was to be left for the needy and the alien to come in and gather grain for food (an interesting system of provision for the poor by welfare work in the field).

So to repeat my question: Why did God wait until the Day of Pentecost for His disciples to be filled with the Holy Spirit and receive power?

Acts 1:4,5,8 – Gathering them together, He commanded them not to leave Jerusalem, but to wait for what the Father had promised, "Which," He said, "you heard of from Me; for John baptized with water, but you will be baptized with the Holy Spirit not many days from now…"but you will receive power when the Holy Spirit has come upon you; and you shall be my witnesses both in Jerusalem, and in all Judea and Samaria, and even to the remotest part of the earth."

Acts 2:1-6; 11, 12, 14 – When the day of Pentecost had come, they were all together in one place. And suddenly there came from heaven a noise like a violent rushing wind, and it filled the whole house where they were sitting. And there appeared to them tongues as of fire distributing themselves, and they rested on each one of them. And they were all filled with the Holy Spirit and began to speak with other tongues, as the Spirit was giving them utterance. Now there were Jews living in Jerusalem, devout men from every nation under heaven. And when this sound occurred, the crowd came together, and were bewildered because each one of them was hearing them speak in his own language…"we hear them in our own tongues speaking of the mighty deeds of God." And they all continued in amazement and great perplexity, saying to one another, "What does this mean?"…But Peter, taking his stand with the eleven, raised his voice and declared to them:…

1. In the Feast of Weeks, thousands of Jewish men were together in Jerusalem, brought together to celebrate the beginning of the new wheat harvest. On the day of Pentecost the disciples were waiting in Jerusalem to

receive Holy Spirit power to be witnesses of the Lord Jesus Christ and begin the New Covenant harvest!

2. In the Feast of Weeks, the first fruits offering of two loaves of bread given for use in the tabernacle/temple was very special. On the day of Pentecost the disciples received Holy Spirit power, manifested by speaking in tongues a proclamation of the mighty deeds of God, in at least fifteen different languages, and then expressed by Peter's sermon, with the immediate first fruits of 3,000 people being saved!

3. In the Feast of Weeks everyone was to be included; even the poorest and most needy of the people were to be remembered and provided for. On the day of Pentecost the disciples received Holy Spirit power to witness to everyone; even people from Samaria and the remotest part of the earth!

I love the beauty of New Testament fulfillment and substance dovetailing with the shadow of Old Testament feast events. Jesus Christ and the implementation of the New Covenant truly fulfilled all prophecy and shadow of the Old Testament.

With you…In you.

When the Lord Jesus Christ walked the earth with His disciples, He was fully man and fully God. So every moment Jesus was with His disciples the Holy Spirit was also with them. When Jesus told His disciples that the Holy Spirit was with them, He was referring to this truth.

When Jesus Christ died on the cross, He paid the penalty for all of mankind's sins. His disciples believed in Him, so at the moment He died on the cross, they became Christians and God was inside of them. When Jesus told His disciples that the Holy Spirit would be in them, He was referring to this truth. How wonderful that from the moment of salvation on, God is inside of every one of us: the Father, the Son, the Holy Spirit. That's the indwelling of the Holy Spirit!

"Thank you Holy Spirit, for being inside of me. I choose to be aware of You, to apprehend You. I open my heart and my mind to better comprehend You. Overwhelm me with Your calm, peace and order."

Chapter Three

WHAT ARE WE WAITING ON?

Tarry ye until you be endued with power

Luke 24:46-49 – *And He said to them, "Thus it is written, that the Christ would suffer and rise again from the dead the third day, and that repentance for forgiveness of sins would be proclaimed in His name to all the nations, beginning from Jerusalem. You are witnesses of these things. And behold, I am sending forth the promise of My Father upon you; but you are to* **stay in the city** *until you are clothed with power from on high."*

Luke 24:49 – (KJV) – And, behold, I send the promise of the Father upon you: but **tarry** *ye in Jerusalem, until you be* ***endued with power*** *from on high.*

Acts 1:4,5,8 – Gathering them together, He commanded them not to leave Jerusalem, but to **wait** *for what the Father had promised, "Which," He said, "you heard of from Me; for John baptized with water, but you will be baptized with the Holy Spirit not many days from now."…but you will receive* **power** *when the Holy Spirit has come upon you; and you shall be my witnesses both in Jerusalem, and in all Judea and Samaria, and even to the remotest part of the earth."*

I was raised in Pentecostal churches, and from my early teen years on, I was taught the doctrine of "tarrying" for the baptism of the Holy Spirit. The teaching was based on a subjective interpretation of the disciples being commanded by Jesus to wait (King James "tarry") in Jerusalem until they received the power of the Holy Spirit. Since they received the power in the experience of being baptized with the Holy Spirit, the teaching concludes that disciples of Jesus need to "tarry" for a time before they receive the baptism of the Holy Spirit.

Here's how the doctrine played out in my life. I accepted Jesus Christ as my Savior during my teen years. The next thing that was emphasized for my Christian walk was to be baptized in water. There was no rush, so a few months later a water baptism was scheduled after the Sunday morning service, and I was baptized, along with one of my church friends. Maybe I didn't pay attention to the instructions, but I remember that it wasn't what I expected. After we were baptized, we traipsed downstairs to the basement men's restroom. As we stripped off our wet clothes, we were cold and quiet. I finally got brave enough to ask my friend a question: "Do you feel any different?" He responded, "No." I paused, feeling empty and confused. Then I said, "Well, it must not have worked." I somehow expected something that would change me inside, so that I wouldn't have to work so hard not to sin. A teenage boy has all kinds of impure thoughts and sins in relating to other people, and I had to work so hard, repenting every week for my sins to be forgiven and to be cleansed. Whatever I thought I should experience or feel, well, it just didn't happen. We finished drying off and changed into dry clothes. And my Christian Pentecostal process continued. Now that I had been saved and baptized in water, it was time for me to complete the trifecta by being baptized with the Holy Spirit.

Here's where the "tarrying" doctrine came into play. It was understood that if you wanted to be baptized with the Holy

WHAT ARE WE WAITING ON?

Spirit, you needed to pray, probably for a long time. It was important to make sure that God understood how important it was to you to receive the Holy Spirit. You did that by long sessions of emotional praying, as you begged God to baptize you with His Spirit. There was a pattern to this prayer quest. Every Sunday night, after the service dismissed, I would go into the prayer room for an afterglow time of prayer. I would confess every sin that I could think of so that the path was clear for the Lord to bless me. Then I would ask to be baptized with the Holy Spirit. And I would ask and ask and ask. I would rend my heart in anguish and cry, but it just seemed like God would not baptize me with the Holy Spirit. I knew I was supposed to tarry, and it would not happen for awhile, but my tarrying went on and on; Sunday after Sunday after Sunday, for months. Other Christians would pray for me; my pastor would lay hands on me; many would speak in tongues all around me, but nothing seemed to be happening. Interestingly enough, I was given very little instruction or teaching, and the many Scriptures about being filled with the Holy Spirit were not covered with me. I was told again and again not to be discouraged; tarrying for the Spirit would take time. I was told to just keep praying and keep asking and keep trying. Once in awhile someone in the prayer room would receive the Holy Spirit and began speaking in tongues. Sometimes it seemed to me like they were faking: they just gave in to the pressure around them and made it up. But there were others who I believed had a genuine experience in being baptized with the Holy Spirit and speaking in tongues. But for me it wasn't happening. I was sincere, I was emotional, I was broken, but it just wasn't happening. This led to me being disillusioned and becoming bitter. I remember sitting in the prayer room, watching other people pray, and being upset with God (dare I say mad at God?). If God didn't want to baptize me with the Holy Spirit, then I didn't want it.

What you hear right now is the precursor to tongues.

One Sunday evening I sat in the prayer room watching my close friend. He was praying and crying and shaking. Something was happening to him. He was saying, "Na-na-na-na-na-na-na." This just kept going on; it seemed like an hour. The pastor sat down beside me and began quietly explaining to me what was happening. "Your friend is getting very close to speaking in tongues. What you hear right now is the precursor to tongues. When he finally lets go and takes hold, he will began to speak in tongues and be baptized with the Holy Spirit. That will eventually happen for you too." To my teen age mind this seemed confusing, complicated and so "not supernatural God." It is true I was becoming bitter, and bitterness is never good. But I will say this: I quickly came to the realization that my bitterness was toward the process and experience. I was bitter about that, but was not bitter toward God. I believed God was supernatural and loving. I began to realize that this doctrine of "tarrying" was not what God wanted. But boy did I get bitter about the process, and as a result of that, became bitter toward my pastor and toward anyone who pushed me to "tarry." I quit going into the prayer room on Sunday nights for afterglow. I told God that if He wanted to baptize me with the Holy Spirit and release power in me, that was great. But I was not going to continue in the anguish of "tarrying."

Over the years I have studied a lot of the twentieth century Pentecostal movement history. There were extraordinary happenings in places like Kansas and California. Reading journals and first person accounts revealed to me Christian disciples that were hungry for more of the Lord. While they didn't know what was missing, they were hungry to be filled with the Spirit. They read about the early church in the book of Acts and began crying out to God for more. More love, more power, more of what God wants. Not knowing exactly what to do, they began praying. For some it was many days and nights of prayer. Then suddenly the Spirit of God would break through and fill them to overflowing. For most of them they began to speak in tongues, as the Spirit gave them utterance. People were letting God have His way, and they were being immersed in His Spirit, and empowered to minister on His behalf. It was extraordinary and it was supernatural.

Now here's the sticking point. It sometimes took a long time to receive this empowering experience from the Lord. The reason: people didn't know what to do in opening up to God, and for some it took quite awhile for them to apprehend God's Spirit within them, comprehend the depth of His love and presence within them, and then allow God to overwhelm the thoughts, emotions and decision-making of their hearts. When individual Christians apprehend and comprehend God within, and then allow Him to overwhelm and immerse their very souls, He moves quickly, providing more love, more power, more wisdom and more Spirit. For many of the seeking people, it took time for them to surrender to God in their very beings. The problem: some people concluded that God had a process, and they just needed to be patient in that process, until He finally opened the floodgates of His Spirit. They actually talked about the necessity of "tarrying" until God would finally move. They saw the delay as an issue of timing, totally in God's hands and beyond their control. They did not see the delay as something happening because of the position and condition of their own hearts. I think these kinds of situations were the beginnings of the teaching about "tarrying." I can understand their hearts in thinking this; I can even understand their commitment to tarrying until they received. It was kind of like Jacob wrestling with God, and not releasing Him until He blessed him. But their conclusions about the necessity of "tarrying" as part of the path and process to receiving the Holy Spirit and speaking in tongues, was not a valid conclusion. What does the Bible say?

Luke 11:13 – "If you then, being evil, know how to give good gifts to your children, how much more will your heavenly Father give the Holy Spirit to those who ask Him?"

> **But it is not mentioned again after this once-off on the day of Pentecost.**

The words of the Lord about tarrying, prior to the day of Pentecost and the disciples being filled with the Holy Spirit and speaking in tongues, were not meant to establish a pattern of prayerful tarrying every time a Christian was to be baptized with the Holy Spirit. It was important to God that the timing of this special event happened when all those men from all over the known earth were gathered in Jerusalem for the one day Feast of Weeks (Pentecost). It happened in the fullness of time, so that thousands could accept the Lord and the witness of the Lord Jesus Christ would have the greatest opportunity for being spread in the world. The disciples had already shown an inclination to go to Galilee, and not stay in Jerusalem where Jesus had been crucified and the religious authorities were ready to persecute all followers of Jesus. So He emphasized to them to wait, stay, tarry, in Jerusalem until they received power from being baptized with the Holy

Spirit. This "tarrying" was a one-time instruction to get the disciples to stay where God wanted them for the Day of Pentecost. It was not to be a doctrinal pattern, repeated every time Christians seek to be baptized with the Holy Spirit. If it was to be a doctrinal pattern, we would see it in the book of Acts, every time someone got baptized with the Holy Spirit. But it is not mentioned again after this once-off on the day of Pentecost.

Isaiah 40:31 – Yes those who wait for the LORD will gain new strength; they will mount up with wings like eagles, they will run and not get tired, they will walk and not become weary.

Waiting for the Lord is a very Biblical concept. Understand that God knows everything and understands what needs to happen and when it needs to happen. He always thinks of what is best for the betterment of His kingdom, and for the purpose of people coming to Him in repentance. So if we wait for the Lord's timing we will enjoy the best for us and for His kingdom. When it comes to the baptism with the Holy Spirit, God's timing is now: the sooner the better for every Christian.

"Lord, I will wait for your timing. I will seek all means to have increased power from you. I thank you that when I ask to be filled with Your Spirit, You will answer quickly and baptize me with Your Holy Spirit."

Chapter Four

THE DAY OF PENTECOST

Speaking and Utterance: Who does what?

*Acts 2:1-4 – When the day of **Pentecost** had come, they were all together in one place. And suddenly there came from heaven a noise like a violent rushing wind, and it filled the whole house where they were sitting. And there appeared to them tongues as of fire distributing themselves, and they rested on each one of them. And **they** were all filled with the Holy Spirit and **began to speak with other tongues**, as the **Spirit was giving them utterance.***

Extraordinary! The Day of Pentecost was here, and the disciples were together in one place in Jerusalem. They did just what Jesus told them, and waited in Jerusalem. They knew something was to happen, and it had to do with the Holy Spirit and power. Suddenly they heard a sound from heaven. It sounded like a very strong wind, the kind that would do damage to buildings and crops. It was very loud and the sound filled the whole house. They saw something resting on each other: it's described as tongues as of fire. I'm not sure what that looks like: maybe real flames on top of their heads? Then they were filled with the Holy Spirit and started speaking in tongues: languages that they didn't know or use. The Spirit gave them utterance and they began to speak in tongues.

Let's refresh our memories about the symbolism (type and shadow) contained in the day of Pentecost. It came to be called Pentecost because it was fifty days after the Feast of Passover. We can sum up the shadow and substance with three words: Harvest, First fruits and Promise.

- **New Covenant harvest.** It is called the Feast of Weeks in the Old Testament, and it was a one day feast in which all Jewish men were to come to the temple in Jerusalem. It was a harvest celebration in which the first fruits of the new wheat harvest were to be dedicated to God. That symbolism was fulfilled in the reality that as the Holy Spirit filled them, they declared the mighty deeds of God in tongues, and preached the gospel to begin the New Covenant harvest of believers for the Lord Jesus Christ.

- **New Covenant first fruits.** In the Feast of Weeks, they were to offer two loaves of leavened bread (fine flour from the wheat) as a special offering of first fruits to God. That symbolism was fulfilled in the declaration of the mighty deeds of God in tongues, and the preaching of the gospel by Peter. The immediate results were the first fruits of the New Covenant: 3,000 people becoming believers in the Lord Jesus Christ.

- **New Covenant promise for all.** In the Feast of Weeks a special proclamation at the big gathering reminded them that everyone, including the poor, the alien and the needy were to be remembered and provided for in the practice of gleaning. The New Covenant gospel was promised to all the people who heard Peter on that day, and promised to their children, and promised to all who were far off; as many as God called to Himself.

Let's look at these "tongues." From the description in Acts chapter two, it is clear that they were languages. There are at least fifteen languages mentioned. A huge crowd gathered together because they heard these disciples of Christ speaking in their own languages from the countries they were born in: There were Parthians, Medes, Elamites, Mesopotamians, Cretans and Arabs. There were men from Judea, Cappadocia, Pontus, Asia, Phrygia, Pamphylia, Egypt, Rome, and parts of Libya around Cyrene. Most of these people were ethnic Jews, but some of them were foreigners who had become Jewish religion participants (proselytes). All of these people were amazed and astonished. Something about the disciples of Christ (probably how they dressed and looked) made the hearers conclude they were common, ignorant Galileans. Yet they were speaking all these languages and declaring the mighty deeds of God. Whaaaaaat? They didn't know what all of this meant, and it really perplexed them. What in the world was happening?

From this description it is clear that earthly languages were being spoken. It is also clear that the disciples were not linguists who spoke many different languages. It was hard enough to communicate in Judea and Galilee, because three different languages were spoken, depending upon who you were talking with: Greek, Aramaic and Hebrew. That was more than enough for the common, regular people to know about languages; forget about them learning other languages existent in the Roman Empire. But God knows all languages and can speak all languages. So the Holy Spirit gave the disciples these words in all these other languages.

Now let's look closely at utterances and speaking. The disciples began speaking in other tongues as the Spirit was giving them utterance. Understanding how this works and how this doesn't work is crucial to every one of us allowing the overwhelming presence of God within us to be manifested in power, signs, wonders, miracles, etc., including speaking in tongues.

The Holy Spirit does not take control of your tongue and wiggle it for you.

1 — The Holy Spirit does not take control of your tongue and wiggle it for you. Just saying that seems ridiculous, but that seems to be the concept that some people have. They think that the Holy Spirit overwhelms their physical body and takes control of their tongue, wiggling it and making sounds that result in a language being spoken that we don't know. They think that if it's really the gift of tongues from the Holy Spirit, then all of the function should be done by God. It should be all of God and none of the human. But that is not what it says in Scripture:

Acts 2:4 – And they were all filled with the Holy Spirit and began to speak with other tongues, as the Spirit was giving them utterance.

The disciples were filled with the Holy Spirit. That was done to them by God. They began to speak in tongues. They were doing the speaking: no Holy Spirit tongue-wiggling. The Spirit was giving them utterance. The Holy Spirit provided the utterance. At no point did the Holy Spirit take control of their tongues.

2 — The Holy Spirit does not need to be primed for the process of speaking in tongues to begin. I have encountered this priming concept in a number of different ways. It happens this way: a Christian wants to be prayed for to receive the

THE DAY OF PENTECOST

baptism of the Holy Spirit. People gather around him and pray for him to be baptized. Nothing seems to be happening, and so someone starts making suggestion to the person:

- "Think of a few syllables and just speak them out loud by faith. Keep speaking them out loud and after awhile the Holy Spirit will take over and you'll be filled with the Holy Spirit."

- "Just start saying "sha na la" or "la la la" (or some other non-sense syllables). Speaking it out loud and strong will show the Holy Spirit that you have faith to be filled, and He will take over and you'll receive the baptism."

- "Start shivering and make sounds when your teeth are chattering. First thing you know, you'll be filled with the Spirit and your language will take off." Seriously, I have had some Christian leaders suggest that the prayer room be kept cold, so that chattering teeth and chattering sounds are easy to make. Then people will be encouraged to speak in tongues.

- "Make something up, by faith. God will honor your faith and give you the gift of tongues."

This is nonsense! It's phony baloney and every time I have heard something like this I am ashamed of God's people. Why do we fall into patterns of "helping" God do His supernatural things? While He is referred to as the "Ancient of Days," He's not an old man that needs help walking and talking. Good grief! We need to stop being immature, grow up and let God be God.

3 — The Holy Spirit does not need us to focus on tongues as the end all and be all. Not once in the book of Acts do we see the disciples seeking tongues or asking for tongues. Tongues did happen, several times, but it looks to be the sovereign choice

and act of God, rather than the aggressive pursuit of a particular gift by Christians. It was cited as evidence that the Holy Spirit had acted, but still it was not pursued as the ultimate goal. In my Pentecostal experience many leaders and fellow saints pursue tongues, rather than pursuing the appropriate Holy Spirit experience. I have actually heard more than one Pentecostal say they are seeking to be filled with tongues! The problem with overemphasizing tongues is that it causes Christians, who want to help in prayer and support, look for tongues or lack of tongues as an indicator that something good has happened, and it can make the seeker feel obligated to "speak in tongues" to please those around him. I have seen several Spirit-filled Christian gather around someone they are praying for, and all speak in tongues. It can turn into a real pressure situation and distract the individual from the full and intimate connection they want and need with the Holy Spirit. My point is this: we should not be seeking tongues; we are to seek the Holy Spirit and power experiences with Him, referred to as baptism, fillings or receivings. As I have been taught by a great spiritual leader: seek the Giver, not the gift. If several Christians are praying together, and several speak in tongues, please be careful that you're not doing it in such a way as to put pressure on someone who isn't speaking in tongues.

But the Holy Spirit did not do the speaking.

The Acts chapter two experience is very clear. The disciples got filled with the Holy Spirit. The promise of the Father was given to them by the Son and they were filled with the Holy Spirit. Allow me to reverse the phrases a little to help us all better understand. (2) the Holy Spirit began giving them utterance; and (1) they began to speak in tongues. In this experience God filled them with the Holy Spirit, and the Holy Spirit began giving them utterance, that is, He gave them words in languages they didn't know. The Holy Spirit placed the words on their spirits. They were aware of the words in their mind and heart. Maybe it was two words to start, or maybe it was more. But the Holy Spirit did not do the speaking. The disciples did. That's exactly how baptism with the Holy Spirit works. The Holy Spirit gives the words, and the individual Christian speaks them out in faith. As he does that the Holy Spirit gives more words. It is a positive manifestation of the wonderful thing that is happening in the individual Christian. The individual is getting in perfect tune with the Spirit of God within. He apprehends God inside, he comprehends all that God is to him and in him, and he surrenders to the Holy Spirit overwhelming his heart; his mind, his emotions and his decision-making. What a blessed thing! In this experience the supernatural power of the Holy Spirit is released and available for the individual to accomplish the work of the ministry. That's what the day of Pentecost experience was all about for the disciples: receiving power when the Holy Spirit came upon them, to be witnesses for Jesus to the whole world. And we are in it for the same reason. The power of the Holy Spirit is to be used in whatever work of the ministry that God wants us to be doing. That's what the baptism of the Holy Spirit is all about: witnessing…ministry… reaching more people for the Lord!

"Lord, help me to trust you with my heart and my soul. I reach in, to take hold of You. I open my being to You and ask You to help me comprehend and know You. I surrender to You. Overwhelm me and fill me, again and again, with Your Holy Spirit. Grant me Your power to use in ministry for Your kingdom."

Chapter Five

THE HOUSE OF CORNELIUS

While Peter was still speaking, the Holy Spirit fell

The Scripture stories from the book of Acts are straightforward and revealing. Luke wrote with a style that almost makes you feel like you were there. I love looking at the stories and using the good sense that God gave me to understand what went on. The story from chapter ten about Peter bringing the gospel message to Cornelius, with both of them getting divine instruction and direction that made it all happen, is fantastic and intriguing!

Cornelius was a Roman centurion, living in Caesarea, who is described as a devout God-fearer. What that means is that he strongly believed in the Jewish religion, and practiced all of it that he could, including much prayer to God, while stopping just short of becoming a Jewish proselyte. If he had become a proselyte, he would have had temple access, just like an ethnic Jew. It is interesting to note that it was the final step he would have had to take that probably kept him from becoming a proselyte: namely, circumcision. Most of the first century proselytes to the Jewish faith were women; they did not have to be circumcised.

An angel appeared to Cornelius in a vision and directed him to send for a man named Simon Peter in the city of Joppa. So he dispatched a three-man team to get Peter. On the next day Peter was up on the rooftop praying, fell into a trance and received a vision from God, repeated three times, that taught him not to call something unclean when God declared it clean. While Peter was pondering the vision, Cornelius's men arrived, asking for Peter. The Holy Spirit told Peter that He Himself had sent the men, and he was to go with them. So Peter, Cornelius's men, and some of the Christian brethren from Joppa, took off for Cornelius's place.

The expectant Cornelius had called together his relatives and friends, many people, and they gathered at his home. Peter said that God had told him to come, and asked Cornelius what it was all about. Cornelius said that God had told him to send for Peter, and they were all ready to hear what God had commanded Peter to say. So Peter preached a great message that clearly spelled out salvation through believing in the Lord Jesus Christ to receive forgiveness of sins. Now let's look at the exact verses:

Acts 10:44-48 – While Peter was still speaking these words, the Holy Spirit fell upon all those who were listening to the message. All the circumcised believers who came with Peter were amazed because the gift of the Holy Spirit had been poured out on the Gentiles also. **For they were hearing them speaking with tongues** *and exalting God. Then Peter answered, "Surely no one can refuse the water for these to be baptized who have received the Holy Spirit just as we did, can he?" And he ordered them to be baptized in the name of Jesus Christ. Then they asked him to stay on for a few days.*

So Peter was still speaking and bang!: the Holy Spirit fell upon this crowd of Gentile relatives and friends. The Jewish Christians who had accompanied Peter from Joppa were amazed: the gift of the Holy Spirit was being poured out on Gentiles! They heard these Gentiles speaking with tongues and exalting God! Peter immediately spoke up: "We need to get these new Christians baptized in water. They have received the Holy Spirit just like we did on the day of Pentecost!" So Peter gave the order and these new Christians were baptized in water, in the name of Jesus Christ. Shortly thereafter, when Peter had returned to Jerusalem, he was called on the carpet by some Jewish Christians because he had eaten with uncircumcised Gentiles. When Peter addressed the issue, he referred to the Holy Spirit experience like this:

Acts 11:15-17 – "And as I began to speak, the Holy Spirit fell upon them just as He did upon us at the beginning. And I remembered the word of the Lord, how He used to say, 'John baptized with water, but you will be baptized with the Holy Spirit. Therefore if God gave to them the same gift as He gave to us also after believing in the Lord Jesus Christ, who was I that I could stand in God's way?"

Maybe more shorter sermons and more Holy Spirit interruptions would be better for the kingdom.

About those long sermons. For all of you long-winded preachers (I include myself: in my heydays of the 80"s my sermons were a little over an hour long, and included the reading of at least twenty Scriptures) you should note that Peter was also long-winded. Take a look at his sermons in Acts chapter two and three. At the house of Cornelius Peter was still speaking when bang!: the Holy Spirit fell on the listening Gentiles. They were baptized with the Holy Spirit and began speaking in tongues and exalting God. When Peter recounted the incident to the Jewish Christians in Jerusalem, he said he began to speak. He was just getting started when he was interrupted by the Holy Spirit. Wouldn't it be nice if the Holy Spirit interrupted us sometimes! Peter had just explained the simple gospel to his Gentile audience. That's exactly what was needed in this situation. I'm being a little tongue in cheek, but maybe more shorter sermons and more Holy Spirit interruptions would be better for the kingdom... you think?

Many labels – same event. Note that this Holy Spirit event is referred to with several different phrases: the Holy Spirit **fell** upon...the **gift** of the Holy Spirit had been **poured out**... **received** the Holy Spirit...**baptized** with the Holy Spirit. This Holy Spirit event that can happen for every Christian is referred to by many different phrases; I have tried to use the phrase "baptism with the Holy Spirit" just so we have a common reference. But there's a lesson here for all of us. Don't get hung up on exact words of phrases. God's Word often uses a number of words or phrases to describe the same event, principle or teaching. Enjoy the fact that all the different phrases will give you a deeper understanding of the concept.

- In the baptism with the Holy Spirit Jesus Christ **baptizes** an individual Christian in His Holy Spirit. His whole being gets immersed in the Spirit of God.

- In the baptism with the Holy Spirit God freely provides a **gift** of His Spirit to an individual Christian. He doesn't have to earn it, buy it or work for it: it's God's gift to him.

- In the baptism with the Holy Spirit, God's Spirit **falls** upon an individual Christian in a strong, decisive and complete way. When His Spirit falls on the individual, it is unexpected and overwhelming, but still very positive.

- In the baptism with the Holy Spirit, an individual Christian **receives** the Holy Spirit from God. God's Spirit is within him, but it takes the individual's act of will to take hold of, embrace and receive the full power of the Holy Spirit.

- In the baptism with the Holy Spirit, God's Spirit is **poured out** upon an individual Christian. The picture is of a liquid flowing all over someone, like water or oil, and the individual gets soaked with the Spirit.

- In the baptism with the Holy Spirit, the individual Christian gets **filled** with the Holy Spirit. Like a container, the individual's body, soul and spirit are filled completely full of the Holy Spirit.

The different words and phrases show us a deep, profound and all-encompassing experience.

Evidence of the event. When this happened at the house of Cornelius, the Jewish Christians were amazed that the Holy Spirit had been poured out on Gentiles! How did they know that the Holy Spirit had been poured out? Peter described it by saying it happened "just as He did upon us at the beginning." All the Jewish Christians saw something that was just like it had been for them back on the day of Pentecost: "For they were hearing them speaking with tongues and exalting God." Speaking in tongues was the physical evidence that happened to them on the day of Pentecost, and it was the physical evidence they were seeing at the house of Cornelius. That's how they could tell that the Gentiles had been baptized with the Holy Spirit.

Here's the straightforward way that it happened. Peter was speaking and clearly explained salvation: everyone who believes in the Lord Jesus Christ receives forgiveness of sins. The Gentiles in the crowd believed at that moment. There was no altar call or sinner's prayer. It simply and clearly happened in their hearts: at that moment they were saved. In the next moment they were baptized with the Holy Spirit and began speaking in tongues and exalting God. I wonder what language they were speaking in tongues – maybe Hebrew? Who knows? So these Gentiles were saved and baptized with the Holy Spirit, and Peter immediately moved to complete the trifecta: let's get them baptized in water, and so that was done. How wonderful!

This is another Scriptural example of disciples being baptized with the Holy Spirit and then speaking in tongues. I point this out so that you can see that baptism with the Holy Spirit and speaking in tongues is a legitimate experience of release and power for Christian disciples.

> Sometimes our prejudices or insecurities
> result in us getting it wrong.

In the 1970's when the charismatic movement was in full swing, all kinds of people from the traditional denominations, especially Catholics, Episcopalians and Presbyterians, seemed to be receiving the gift of the Holy Spirit, exercising many of the gifts of the Spirit, including speaking in tongues and prophesying. Some of the Pentecostals were very uncertain and uncomfortable about this, because they didn't think these denominational people were even saved, or had the correct

THE HOUSE OF CORNELIUS

understanding of the Biblical doctrine of salvation. Pentecostals should have paid more attention to the events recorded in Acts chapter eleven about the house of Cornelius. God knows who is really saved, and who isn't. When He gives His gift of the Holy Spirit to people, it's because they are already saved. The Holy Spirit doesn't get it wrong, but sometimes our prejudices or insecurities result in us getting it wrong. When Peter and the Jewish Christians saw these Gentiles get baptized with the Holy Spirit, they decided to be in agreement with the Holy Spirit. "Let's get these new Christians baptized!"

"Lord, I am so thankful that You quickly and freely give us salvation and baptism with the Holy Spirit. You don't make it a mystery; You don't require any special gimmicks from us; You don't make us jump through special hoops. You simply respond to our choice to believe, to be open and to receive. Thank you Jesus!"

Chapter Six

DISCIPLES IN EPHESUS

Did you receive the Holy Spirit when you believed?

*Acts 19:1-6 – It happened that while Apollos was at Corinth, Paul passed through the upper country and came to Ephesus, and found some disciples. He said to them, "Did you receive the Holy Spirit when you believed?" And they said to him, "No, we have not even heard whether there is a Holy Spirit." And he said, "Into what then were you baptized?" And they said, "Into John's baptism." Paul said, "John baptized with the baptism of repentance, telling the people to believe in Him who was coming after him, that is, in Jesus." When they heard this, they were baptized in the name of the Lord Jesus. And when Paul had laid his hands upon them, the Holy Spirit came on them, and **they began speaking in tongues and prophesying.** There were in all about twelve men.*

I love this story of Paul encountering some disciples in Ephesus. It begs us to ask questions, and that is exactly what we will do. From chapter eighteen we learn that Paul had started on his third missionary journey. He passed through the regions of Galatia and Phrygia, strengthening all the disciples. Now before he got to Ephesus, we are told what was happening in Ephesus with Apollos, Priscilla and Aquila. This is important because it gives us the setting and background for Paul's encounter with some disciples when he gets to Ephesus.

Apollos was a Jewish man who had been born in Alexandria. He was a very eloquent speaker who knew the Old Testament Scriptures very well. He had been instructed in the way of the Lord, and because he had such a fervent spirit about the things of the Lord, he taught and preached, **accurately,** the things concerning Jesus. But something was amiss: he was only **acquainted with the baptism of John**. He spoke boldly in the synagogue, combining his knowledge of the message of John the Baptist with his strong grasp and understanding of the Old Testament Scriptures. It was a true message, but was not complete because he didn't yet know about Jesus.

Priscilla and Aquila were a married couple who had been expelled from Rome under the decree of Emperor Claudius (He expelled all the Jews from Rome). They settled in Corinth, and that's where they met Paul, when he came to spread the gospel. They became the nucleus of the church, and Paul lived with them for about 1½ years, sometimes making tents, but always with the primary mission of preaching the gospel. Paul decided to return to Syria and as he began the journey, he took Priscilla and Aquila with him. They stopped briefly in Ephesus, where Paul had the opportunity to reason with the Jews in the synagogue. The Jews asked Paul to stay around for awhile, but he declined. He did leave Priscilla and Aquila in Ephesus, but he set sail from Ephesus to continue his journey back to Syria. One day Priscilla and Aquila heard Apollos speaking in the synagogue of Ephesus. Remember he was some kind of special speaker; eloquent, bold and very knowledgeable of Old Testament Scripture. It seems incredible to me that he was able to preach accurately the things concerning Jesus, since he was only acquainted with the baptism of John. I think that

DISCIPLES IN EPHESUS

somehow Apollos had heard the message of John the Baptist, with the emphasis upon repentance and the soon coming Messiah. Being in Alexandria he was not exposed to the actual ministry and message of Jesus. It was as though he had been told it was time for repentance and preparation for the coming Messiah, and then being isolated in Alexandria, he did an excellent job of applying the Old Testament Scripture to the message of expectation for the coming Messiah. Anyway Priscilla and Aquila took him aside, and explained the way of God more accurately to him. It gave him a truly complete understanding of the Lord Jesus Christ. Shortly thereafter, he traveled across to Corinth, where the church was already established. He was a real help to the Christian disciples because he easily refuted the Jews who were arguing against Jesus, and did it using their own Scriptures to prove that Jesus was the Christ.

> **They were disciples and believers, even though they had not heard the full gospel of the Lord Jesus Christ.**

So the situation in Ephesus is that there were some Jewish believers who had heard the gospel from Paul, but since he only ministered briefly there, there were other disciples who had only heard the message of the coming Messiah that John the Baptist had preached. Probably they had heard it through the speaking of Apollos, and they were disciples and believers, even though they had not heard the full gospel of the Lord Jesus Christ. Enter Paul, back on the scene.

I looked carefully at the questions Paul asked in this story and I kept asking myself, "Why would he ask that? What's the full story here?" After considering the answers from these disciples and the context of the previous chapter in Acts, I think the story went like this:

> ## "No, we haven't even heard whether there is a Holy Spirit."

When Paul arrived back in town he found some disciples and was praying with them. It's always a good time when you can pray together with the brethren. As they were praying, Paul did what he would regularly do; sometimes praying in the common language, sometimes praying in tongues. This was something new to these disciples, this praying in tongues, so I imagine they were looking kind of funny at Paul. When Paul noticed their questioning looks, he could tell that they weren't used to hearing someone speak in tongues. And if they hadn't heard someone speaking in tongues before, they had not yet experienced the joy and release of being baptized with the Holy Spirit. For if they had been baptized with the Holy Spirit, they would have spoken with tongues, and hearing him speak in tongues in prayer would not have been strange to them. So he asked them, "Did you receive the Holy Spirit when you believed?" (I would paraphrase it like this: "Were you baptized with the Holy Spirit when you believed in the Lord?" So they responded to his question: "No, we haven't even heard whether there is a Holy Spirit." Now Paul is trying to figure out how they couldn't have heard of the Holy Spirit. New Christians were baptized in water, "in the name of the Father, and the Son, and the Holy Spirit, the Lord Jesus Christ." If they hadn't heard about the Holy Spirit at water baptism, how were they baptized? So he asked, "Into what then were you baptized?" They responded, "Into John's baptism." Now Paul began to understand what was going on. This was a group of disciples who were believers in the coming Messiah, as John had said, "the one who was coming after him." So Paul told them who the coming Messiah was, and the name of the one that came after John: namely Jesus. They were already believers in their Savior and Lord, and now they knew his name. So they immediately got baptized in water by Paul; in the name of the Father, and the Son, and the Holy Spirit, the Lord Jesus Christ. Paul then laid hands on them, praying for them to be baptized with the Holy Spirit. The Holy Spirit came on them and they began speaking in tongues and prophesying. It must have been a loud time of prayer, because there were twelve of them.

This is another Scriptural example of disciples being baptized with the Holy Spirit and then speaking in tongues. I point this out so that you can see that baptism with the Holy Spirit and speaking in tongues is a legitimate experience of release and power for Christian disciples.

Notice also the two different phrases used to describe this baptism with the Holy Spirit: "received the Holy Spirit," and "the Holy Spirit came on them." Remember the lesson that this teaches us. Don't get hung up on exact words of phrases. God's Word often uses a number of words or phrases to describe the same event, principle or teaching. Enjoy the fact that all the different phrases will give you a deeper understanding of the concept.

"Lord I rejoice that you honor our hearts of belief, even though we only know in part, or only have half the picture.

Our salvation and subsequent experiences in the Holy Spirit are not dependent upon our understanding, but wholly provided for by your love and grace. Thank you for saving me and baptizing me with your Holy Spirit by faith."

Chapter Seven

MY BAPTISM WITH THE HOLY SPIRIT

The deal I made with God

> Here was my deal with God:
> I was willing to be baptized with the Holy Spirit,
> but only if there were no 'tongues.'

Let me subjectively share my personal experience of being baptized with the Holy Spirit as a 17-year old. As I have shared with you, I had been introduced to the practice of tarrying for the baptism with the Holy Spirit. Here's where the "tarrying" doctrine came into play. It was understood that if you wanted to be baptized with the Holy Spirit, you needed to pray, probably for a long time. It was important to make sure that God understood how important it was to you to receive the Holy Spirit. You did that by long sessions of emotional praying, as you begged God to baptize you with His Spirit. There was a pattern to this prayer quest. Every Sunday night, after the service dismissed, I would go into the prayer room for an afterglow time of prayer. I would confess every sin that I could think of so that the path was clear for the Lord to bless me. Then I would ask to be baptized with the Holy Spirit. And I would ask and ask and ask. I would rend my heart in anguish and cry, but it just seemed like God would not baptize me with the Holy Spirit. I knew I was supposed to tarry, and it would not happen for while, but my tarrying went on and on; Sunday after Sunday after Sunday, for months. Other Christians would pray for me; my pastor would lay hands on me; many would speak in tongues all around me, but nothing seemed to be happening. Interestingly enough, I was given very little instruction or teaching, and the many Scriptures about being filled with the Holy Spirit were not covered with me. I was told again and again not to be discouraged; tarrying for the Spirit would take time. I was told to just keep praying and keep asking and keep trying. Once in awhile someone in the prayer room would receive the Holy Spirit and began speaking in tongues. Sometimes it seemed to me like they were faking: they just gave in to the pressure around them and made it up. But there were others who I believed had a genuine experience in being baptized with the Holy Spirit and speaking in tongues. But for me it wasn't happening. I was sincere, I was emotional, I was broken, but it just wasn't happening. This led to me being disillusioned and becoming bitter. I remember sitting in the prayer room, watching other people pray, and being upset with God (dare I say mad at God?). If God didn't want to baptize me with the Holy Spirit, then I didn't want it. It is true I was becoming bitter, and bitterness is never good. But I will say this: I quickly came to the realization that my bitterness was toward the process and experience. I was bitter about that, but was not bitter toward God. I believed God was supernatural and loving. I began to realize that this doctrine of "tarrying" was not what God wanted. But boy did

MY BAPTISM WITH THE HOLY SPIRIT

I get bitter about the process, and as a result of that, became bitter toward my pastor and toward anyone who pushed me to "tarry." I quit going into the prayer room on Sunday nights for afterglow. I told God that if He wanted to baptize me with the Holy Spirit and release power in me, that was great. But I was not going to continue in the anguish of "tarrying." I talked this over with God several times. As a teenager, my talks with God were a whole lot of me talking, and probably not listening. At any rate I came up with an understanding with God. Here was my deal with God: I was willing to be baptized with the Holy Spirit, but only if there were no 'tongues.' He could do it whenever He wanted to, and I would receive it gladly. But until then I wasn't going to worry about it in any way, shape or form. I felt set free, relaxed and embraced by a loving God. I do have to say that I was the one who formed the "understanding." As I think back, I can't recall any point that God said "O.K." to the agreement. But I digress.

One week-end in the early summer I took a road trip with my friend Johnny. I think Johnny was a nephew of a foster brother of my sister-in-law. He was a little younger than me, maybe sixteen. Since I had a reputation as a "hood" prior to becoming a Christian, Johnny and I got along well. I was really impressed with Johnny's courage in life. He was a diabetic, who had to administer insulin shots to himself each day. To me it took guts and courage to give yourself a shot in the belly each day. Although I had been a teenage brawler and fighter, I couldn't even watch Johnny giving himself the shot without getting sick. I had made a fresh commitment of my life to the Lord several months earlier, and had a lot of changing going on in my life. At any rate we took off from Portland, OR in my 1961 Ford, and drove down to Tillamook, OR. Tillamook was a semi-beach town, a few miles away from the Oregon Coast. I had visited the town a few months before as part of a youth group on an evangelistic ministry trip. On that visit there was a young man (named Mike, if I remember) who had committed his life to Christ. He and I had maintained contact, and I did my best to help him in his walk with the Lord. So we connected in Tillamook to knock around and do what teenage boys do. Part of it was chasing girls; part of it was talking about things happening in our lives. Mike was definitely a Christian, but he was struggling with stopping pornography and smoking practices. He was discouraged and really wanted God to deliver him. I also shared with him that I wanted us to do our best to lead Johnny to the Lord.

Early Sunday morning God awakened me with what I can only describe as a "word of faith" for the day. He impressed strongly on me that three things were going to happen that day: 1-Johnny was going to accept Jesus Christ as his Savior and Lord; 2-Mike was going to be delivered from his pornography and smoking addictions; and 3-I was going to be baptized with the Holy Spirit. Now I was a "cool" young Christian man; not given to imagination or weirdness. Other teens did weird spiritual things, but not me. Yet I knew that I knew that I knew God had spoken to me. I shared this faith word with Mike, and he wanted to believe. But I could tell he was thinking I was becoming weird. The three of us attended Sunday morning services at the local Assembly of God church. The pastor had an altar call at the end of his Sunday morning service, but Johnny did not respond to it, and didn't seem to be affected by anything spiritual. He and I spent the afternoon driving to the beach, and figuring out how to get some food. We were pretty much out of money and food (typical poor boy road trip). We stopped by one girl's house and she gave us half a chocolate cake. We took it to the local park and wolfed it down: half for me and half for Johnny. I shudder to think what that did to his insulin levels, but he took

MY BAPTISM WITH THE HOLY SPIRIT

his regular shot and seemed unaffected. I remained full of faith: convinced that God had told me those three things.

When evening came around, Johnny and I met up with Mike and went back to the church for an evening service. At the conclusion of the sermon, once again the pastor gave an altar call. This time around Johnny was listening and went forward to receive Christ. The pastor invited others to come forward for prayer, and it was a special, powerful spiritual time. Mike went forward and several people laid hands on him and were praying strongly for him. I also went forward, to observe, and to rejoice with people. In one magical moment Mike looked over at me, and gave me a strong nod. I knew what it meant: God had delivered him; he had been set free from his addictions by the power of God. I was so happy and full of joy. I turned to face forward and started to say, "God, I love you." At that moment the power of the Holy Spirit fell on me and I began speaking in tongues! A lot of speaking in tongues. For a long period, maybe thirty minutes I was speaking in tongues: it seemed like I was praising God, but I didn't understand any of it. But it was wonderful! As the afterglow prayer time began to break up, people were hugging each other and saying their good-byes for the night. I remember a couple of girls coming over and telling me good-bye. I responded, still speaking in tongues! Mike came over and gave me a big hug, then said good-bye for the week-end. I tried to tell him good-bye, but I was still speaking in tongues! Johnny came over to hug me and tell me how happy he was with Jesus. I wanted to respond positively and let him know I was happy too, but what came out of my mouth was still speaking in tongues! I couldn't seem to speak English. Johnny and I left the building, got into my old Ford, and started the 1½ hour trip back to Portland. As we were driving Johnny was talking to me, but all I could respond with was more speaking in tongues. Finally I tried super hard and got a couple of English words out. Slowly I returned to being able to control my words and speak in English. It had been about 1 hour and 15 minutes that I had spoken only tongues as the Spirit gave me utterance. And it was a lot of words in some language I didn't know. Johnny actually enjoyed how powerfully the Holy Spirit had gotten hold of me, because he was on an emotional high, precipitated by his salvation. We sang songs and rejoiced all the way back to Portland. Even though Johnny didn't know the songs he still sang with gusto. What a day! What a night! Full of faith, full of power and full of the Holy Spirit.

> **I didn't want to have anything to do with speaking in tongues.**

As I have looked back over the years, I have asked myself why God did it that way for me. My theory is that it was God's answer to my "understanding" with him. I didn't want to have anything to do with speaking in tongues, but He wanted to do it "the Bible way." I guess He had never agreed to my deal! No matter what I have thought at times over the last 48 years, I have never doubted that when I was baptized with the Holy Spirit I had spoken in tongues. It was totally God: not me, not pressure from others, not tarrying doctrine. It was up and up, all the way, God.

Baptism with the Holy Spirit is an expectation and experience taught by the Bible. It involves all of the Godhead; it is promised to believers by the Father, it is an action taken by Jesus, that John the Baptist predicted concerning the expected coming Messiah (Christ, the Anointed One), and it is accomplished by the Holy Spirit in the life and heart of every Christian believer. As you consider these summary points, put it in the first person; put yourself in the driver's seat:

- I am wheat; I am not chaff! Lord, bless me by baptizing me with your Holy Spirit. Don't judge me by baptizing me with fire. I choose to be baptized, not burned!

- The Holy Spirit abides in me from the moment I become a Christian. Then through apprehending God, understanding Him and opening my being to being overwhelmed by His Spirit, I get submerged (baptized) in the Holy Spirit.

- The baptism with the Holy Spirit is a special release of God's power in me and through me, for witnessing and ministering the gospel and glory of the Lord Jesus Christ.

- Speaking in tongues is the initial sign and evidence of being baptized with the Holy Spirit. It is clearly expressed on the disciples at the Day of Pentecost, on the brand new disciples in the house of Cornelius, and on the disciples in Ephesus.

- The Holy Spirit will give me the utterance of tongues, and I will speak them by faith. The Holy Spirit gives the utterance; I speak it!

I suggest you pray and ask God to baptize you with the Holy Spirit. I encourage you to get together with some Christian friends who believe in this experience and have the faith to pray in agreement with you. Jesus will baptize you with His Holy Spirit and you will speak in tongues as His Spirit gives you words. It may be a few words, or many, but take the step of faith and speak them out. It is real, it is God, and it is good for you!

Set aside your doubts and fears. Don't be distracted or deterred by your preconceptions or by previous teachings to the contrary. The teachings, gifts and experiences outlined in the New Testament are valid for every Christian today. Embrace the baptism with the Holy Spirit, and be empowered in the name of the Lord Jesus Christ.

Part Two

Speaking in Tongues - For Edification

"I thank God, I speak in tongues more than you all."

I Corinthians 14:18

Chapter Eight

IT'S GOOD FOR YOU!

Not to be feared, fought or forbidden

I pray in tongues a lot, and have for the last 48 years of my Christian life. That spiritual practice has helped build me up, and move in concert with what the Lord wants me to be doing. In the first few years I didn't think about the people around me in the church service, crowd or community, so some of what I did in praying and ministering was out of order and did not build up the people around me. After I moved out of a traditional Pentecostal denomination, I began to receive some Bible teaching that opened my eyes and changed my personal practices, as well as my own ministry and teaching. Over the last thirty-five years I have been more sensitive to what the Holy Spirit wants, and so I have strived to benefit from the gift of speaking in tongues, but to do it in a Biblical way, so that it was decent, orderly and built up everyone. Without apology I am letting you know that I pray in tongues a lot and I believe the gift and benefits are also available for every Christian, and can be exercised in a decent and orderly way that builds up everyone.

In our modern days speaking in tongues has become an oddity to the Christian community. Those who do speak in tongues are almost embarrassed about it. They don't want to "force it" onto anyone else; they are private about it; so much so that they are almost apologetic about speaking in tongues or even believing in it. In fact, for some tongues speakers they are almost ashamed of it. Churches and denominations that believed strongly in the gift and doctrine of tongues have softened their presentation of the belief, to the point that you can barely uncover what they believe or practice. Back in the 70's and 80's non-denominational churches would proudly proclaim that they were charismatic, whereas nowadays I have heard more than one pastor say something like this: "We're not Pentecostal or charismatic. We are balanced Bible believers." The implication is that Pentecostals and charismatics are not balanced. Why would that be, if speaking in tongues is sound Biblical doctrine?

Let me share from my personal experiences. I have been a part of over twenty Pentecostal and charismatic churches in my lifetime, and have visited many more, and I have seen a lot: a lot of good, Holy Spirit-powered things, and a lot of not so good actions, practices and teachings.

Some people fake tongues. Oh no! That's terrible! If tongues can be faked how can anyone trust the gift of tongues? The simple answer is that the Holy Spirit knows when a human fakes tongues, and He does what needs to be done, so that His will and purpose do not get thwarted. For example, the gift of distinguishing of spirits helps sincere Christians know what spirit is behind something. That gift of the Spirit is a safeguard against things falsely attributed to the Holy Spirit.

Why would someone fake speaking in tongues?

Then the more important question to ask is this: why would someone fake speaking in tongues? More than once I have heard instances of people just making fun of Pentecostals and charismatics: "Shama-lama-ding-dong-shundali." The sad truth is that some writers, movie makers and just regular people make fun of all kinds of spiritual things, and that's unfortunate. Such is human nature. But making fun of something doesn't make it untrue. Another reason someone might fake speaking in tongues is peer pressure, or desire to please. This is a problem more difficult to acknowledge, but sadly it can be true. If someone is asking God to baptize them with the Holy Spirit, and they know that they are expected to speak in tongues, but they can't seem to do it, they can begin to feel pressure. If they are praying with a group of believers and those around them are speaking in tongues, they can feel pressure to do the same thing. The reality is this: we Pentecostal/charismatic Christians need to minister the baptism with the Holy Spirit to other believers in such a way that it is all about the power of God, and not in any way about what we expect the individual to do. We need to instruct with the Word of God, pray in love over individuals, counsel carefully to avoid pressure or expectations and allow God to be God without any human influence. People can be susceptible to manipulation, and we must remove any of that from our ministry and instruction. I have seen pressure, manipulation and, at times, intimidation from Christian leaders, and God never intended that His leaders do that.

I Peter 5:2 – shepherd the flock of God among you, exercising oversight not under compulsion, but voluntarily, according to the will of God;...

People do goofy things and call them "Holy Spirit" things. Because the gifts of the Spirit, including speaking in tongues, are experiences people have, they tend to attract people who love having experiences. And people who love experiences tend to feed off the positive emotions they feel with those experiences. In other words I have seen a lot Pentecostals and charismatics chase after experiences that give them good emotional feelings. They chase after whatever new experience is happening, and mimic it, thinking that is the right thing to do. Someone somewhere is touched by the Holy Spirit, and begins laughing a lot for a long period of time. That is the individual's emotional reaction to being touched by the Holy Spirit. But they think the laughing is the Holy Spirit's doing. Then others see the laughing or hear about it and start laughing to try and get the same experience. People began calling it "laughing in the Spirit." A whole new movement starts happening as hundreds, then thousands of people begin laughing in the Spirit. Or someone is praying at the altar after the service and the Holy Spirit touches them strongly and they fall down flat on the ground, still praying and just loving on God. Other people see it and put a label on it: "slain in the Spirit," or "falling in the Spirit." And a whole new movement starts happening as hundreds, then thousands of people begin falling in the Spirit.

Many years ago when I was in the army, I was attending a service at a small independent Pentecostal church in the San Antonio area. I had accompanied a lady that I had met at a downtown mission. The congregation was singing praise songs and went into a free praise time. Some people were shouting; some were speaking in tongues, others were dancing around. Suddenly the lady that I had come with began screaming – blood curdling shrieks and screams, just like you would hear in the horror movies. It made the hairs on the back of my neck stand up. I was quietly observing everyone; it was a wild scene. No one seemed to be reacting to the screaming at all. Things finally calmed down and the service ended. When we had exited the building I asked the lady I was with what had happened when she started screaming.

Quite matter of factly she said, "Oh. I was screaming in the Spirit. The Holy Spirit just does that to me." Now you may be thinking to yourself: "It was a demon. She was demon-possessed." I don't think so. She and I had talked clearly about our personal salvation/conversion experiences.

So what is this all about? It sounds crazy and goofy. Falling in the Spirit? Laughing in the Spirit? Screaming in the Spirit? Here is what can happen to genuine Christians.

1. The individual sincerely reaches out to apprehend the Holy Spirit, and it is powerful when God responds!

2. The individual has a deep response from the emotional part of their soul; that often has a physical effect. The falling, the laughing, the dancing, the screaming is a reaction of their own soul: an emotional and/or physical reaction. But it is their soul, their emotions, their physical body doing the thing…not the Holy Spirit.

3. The individual (or others who see the happening or hear about the happening) assigns their emotional reaction or physical reaction to the Holy Spirit, deciding that the feeling or experience is the Holy Spirit. Thus is born laughing in the Spirit, or being slain in the Spirit, or screaming in the Spirit.

4. Other individual Christians buy into the incorrect conclusion that the individual's reaction (physical and/or emotional) is a Holy Spirit thing, and so they start imitating whatever the "thing" is, trying to get the same Holy Spirit touch.

What I have just described is not sound doctrine based upon the word of God.

> If it feels good, it must be the Holy Spirit
> and it must be truth.

If it feels good, it must be the Holy Spirit and it must be truth. This is exactly the same as the worldly doctrine: it can't be wrong if it feels so right…if it feels good do it!

People see weird things, think it's crazy and withdraw from Holy Spirit things. Paul actually mentions this very happening in I Corinthians.

I Corinthians 14:23 – Therefore if the whole church assembles together and all speak in tongues, and ungifted men or unbelievers enter, will they not say that you are mad?

Paul was addressing the Corinthian church, in which too much speaking in tongues was going on, and Christians were not being decent or in order, and instead of trying to build everyone up, they were inconsiderate of others. He gave them good instruction on how to come back into balance by pointing out the obvious. "People are going to think you're all a bunch of whackos."

Acts 2:13 – But others were mocking and saying, "They are full of sweet wine."

On the day of Pentecost Christian disciples, newly baptized with the Holy Spirit, manifested the extraordinary gift of speaking in tongues: at least fifteen different languages speaking of the mighty deeds of God. It was supernatural; it was divinely powerful; yet there were people who scoffed and mocked, calling it a manifestation of drunkenness.

The genuine manifestations of the Holy Spirit can look really weird to people. When that happens, we need to do our best to explain Bible things to them, and trust the convincing influence of the Holy Spirit will help them accept the true things of God. The phony manifestations of our human body and soul should not be attributed to the Holy Spirit. In our thinking and our presentation before other people, we need to be wise as serpents, but innocent as doves.

Should we limit Holy Spirit power manifestations to the first century? The single biggest way in which people withdraw from the Holy Spirit is by relegating and limiting His powerful things to the first century church. If they can teach that the miracles and gifts of the first century apostolic church were limited to the first century, and are not for the church today, that allows them to ignore all of the New Testament teachings about the things of the Spirit. And that is exactly what they do.

As a teenager I bounced back and forth between a Pentecostal church and a Baptist church. The Pentecostal church seemed full of life, but emotionally and experientially out of balance. The Baptist church seemed solid, but very dry and non-emotional. A prayer meeting at the Pentecostal church was lively and often loud and emotional. A prayer meeting at the Baptist church was like a tomb: total silence and non-movement. The Pentecostals would warn me against the Baptist because they denied the power of the Spirit. The Baptists would warn me against the Pentecostals because they were super emotional and faking things. One thing stood out strongly to me: their opposing stances on supernatural healing. The Pentecostals believed divine healing was possible and they would pray for people to be healed: and some people were healed. I saw it. The Baptists believed divine healing was not possible because it was limited to the first century church. So they would not pray for people to be healed. One very sad experience stands out in my mind. I won't share the details, but suffice it to say that one of the leading deacons in the Baptist church, that I respected a lot, shared his view on divine healing with me by telling a sad, almost crude joke that repeated this punch line several times: "He fell over; he's a cripple you know." That deacon lost a lot of respect in my eyes when he told the joke. As I think about it years later, I think it was his attempt to deal with the doctrine he had been taught: that divine healing was not for today.

Let me address this doctrine face on.

I Corinthians 13:8-10 – Love never fails; but if there are gifts of prophecy, they will be done away; if there are tongues, they will cease; if there is knowledge, it will be done away. For we know in part and we prophesy in part; but when the perfect comes, the partial will be done away. When I was a child, I used to speak like a child, reason like a child; when I became a man, I did away with childish things. For now we see in a mirror darkly, but then face to face; now I know in part, but then I will know fully just as I also have been fully known. But now faith, hope, love, abide these three; but the greatest of these is love.

The Christians who teach the doctrine that the gifts of the Spirit are not for today base it on this passage from I Corinthians thirteen. They teach that the gifts of the Spirit are in part, or partial. They say that when the perfect comes, all the gifts of the Spirit will be done away, and they teach that "when the perfect comes" refers to the completion of the writing of the New Testament scriptures. Since the New Testament was completely written in the first century, and it is perfect (after all, it is the infallible Word of God), the perfect came a long time ago. So prophecy is done away; tongues has ceased; words of knowledge are done away; all the gifts of the Spirit have ceased and are done away. As grown up Christians we are no longer speaking or acting like children. If there are people in the present who say that they are exercising the gifts of the Holy Spirit, they are either lying, or are deceived by Satan. Leaders who teach that the gifts of the Holy Spirit are for today are false teachers. The perfect has come, so the gifts of the Holy Spirit are no longer needed. That's the "doctrine" that they use to deny the gifts and power of the Holy Spirit for today.

This doctrine is wrong. "When the perfect comes" refers to the time when we are face to face with the Lord; either at our physical death, or at the Second Coming of Christ. It does not refer to the writing of the New Testament Scripture. If we simply look at this Scripture we can see that. "For now we see in a mirror darkly, but then face to face; now I know in part; but then I will know fully, just as I also have been fully known." No Christian living today can say that he knows fully just as he is fully known (only God knows us fully). Every Christian living today can say that he sees as though he's looking into a darkened mirror. So the perfect has not come yet. We will see everything clearly and know everything fully when Jesus returns and we see him "face to face." The key to correctly interpreting this passage of Scripture is in that phrase "face to face." This is easy to understand if you read the passage of the Scripture in context. You cannot deny the gifts and power of the Holy Spirit are for today by saying that the perfect has come. If you have been taught this incorrect doctrine, open your heart to the guidance of the Spirit of Truth and see if He reveals the correct interpretation to you.

Why do they need to deny the gifts and power of the Holy Spirit are for today? I believe it is because they have seen the mistakes and excess that have happened in the Pentecostal and charismatic circles, and they want to run as far away from it as possible. As my mother used to say: they have decided to throw out the baby with the bath water. So they hide behind this doctrine, even though it is incorrect interpretation of Scripture. I have tried to discuss this very doctrine with some of my Christian brethren who deny the gifts and power of the Holy Spirit for today, and I have been met with resistance and denial, but no willingness to see the obvious meaning of this Scripture, in context.

I invite you to come with me as we look at what the Bible says about speaking in tongues. In a simple and straightforward way let's examine the Scriptures. Let's avoid all the hoopla, emotions and "experience-grabbing." Let's learn how the Holy Spirit wants things done: decently and in order, and in the best way to build up everyone. Consider with me that speaking in tongues is good for every Christian; yes, that it's good for you. Allow the Holy Spirit to speak to you about what His Word really means.

Chapter Nine

SEVEN GEMS FROM I CORINTHIANS 14
Instruction for the Charismatic Corinthian Congregation

We are privileged to have all the information we do about the church in Corinth. Paul had ministered there for a little over 1½ years. Aquila and Priscilla were an important part of the congregation, and Paul had lived with them, at times making tents with them for a living; at times spending all his time evangelizing and building the church. Paul had left Corinth to minister to other parts of Europe and Asia. About five years later he wrote two lengthy epistles back to the church there. In those letters he dealt with a lot of the inner workings of this local church, including relationships, services and ordinances. We know more about this Corinthian congregation because of those letters. Many of the human frailties and weaknesses that Christians of any congregation might have are revealed in the Corinthian church.

The congregation was acting in an indecent, disorderly and selfish way.

In I Corinthian chapters 12-14 a picture is painted of this very "charismatic" congregation. The Corinthians loved the gifts and power of the Holy Spirit; but their personal enjoyment and feelings seemed to dominate what they practiced. Paul picks their misuse of the gift of speaking in tongues as the example to teach them proper emphasis and use of the gifts of the Holy Spirit. From Paul's comments and instructions we can see that many of them spoke in tongues a lot. And while it was fun, encouraging, uplifting and edifying for many individuals, it was being practiced in such a way that the plans and purposes of God, in the use of the gifts of the Spirit, were being thwarted, twisted and abused. The congregation was acting in an indecent, disorderly and selfish way, that brought confusion, division and was even driving some people away from the things of the Spirit, the church and even the gospel. So Paul gave them instruction that helps us see how valuable the gifts of the Spirit are, and how to use them in a decent, orderly way that builds up everyone. That's what we want: not to forbid the gifts, but to use them correctly; just as God intends.

In Chapter 12 Paul addresses spiritual things, especially spiritual gifts of the Spirit. Since Paul had spent so much time as part of this congregation, he had undoubtedly led and guided them in proper, edifying conduct as a congregation. But it had been five years and a lot of things can happen in a church in that time period. To build the proper foundation for his instruction and correction Paul reviewed the basics, reminding the Corinthians of how the body of Christ functions, and how everyone is important and essential. He reminded them of the key gifts of the Spirit, and left them with this pivotal and instructional command: "But earnestly desire the greater gifts."

I have to insert an important parenthetical comment here. In the I Corinthians letter Paul points the congregation to the gift of prophecy as a better gift for their situation. So people have concluded that prophecy is one of the greater gifts that we all need to earnestly desire. That's an incorrect assumption; it presumes more than Paul intended. Paul taught the general principles of balance, decency, order and "other-edification" as the priorities in the exercise of spiritual gifts. For the Corinthian church, and their specific imbalanced situation, he gave this specific instructional application: less speaking in tongues and more speaking prophecy. Prophecy was definitely one of the greater gifts that the Corinthians needed to earnestly desire, in order to come back into balance and order in their specific situation. For all of us, before we fixate on certain special gifts to earnestly desire, we need to evaluate what will bring our specific church and our specific lives into balance. For all of us, the greater gifts we are to earnestly desire are the ones that help us walk in balance, order, decency and other-edification. Now back to our main topic.

In chapter 13 Paul sets out the priority motivation for everything we do and especially for how and why we minister the gifts of the Spirit. And he does it in the greatest love chapter in the Bible. Love abides as the greatest and most important motive as we move to do what the Holy Spirit wants us to do.

In chapter 14 Paul specifically addresses the gifts of the Spirit in the context of the church service. There are times that the Holy Spirit wants us to exercise His gifts outside of church services, and these gifts help bring people to a saving knowledge of the Lord Jesus Christ. But the gifts are also used within the body of Christ, and in our church services. This chapter teaches us proper church service conduct, especially with regard to the gifts of the Spirit. We are to make balance, decency, order and other-edification the priority in our church service conduct. That being said, Paul makes several statements in this chapter that give us insight and understanding into the gift of speaking in tongues, and we want to weigh those things as we consider my unapologetic encouragement to all of you: speaking in tongues — it's good for you!

I Corinthians 14:2 – For one who speaks in a tongue does not speak to men but **to God***; for no one understands, but in his spirit he speaks* **mysteries.**

Insight #1 – When one speaks in tongues, he speaks mysteries.

Since other humans around the tongues speaker do not understand the language being spoken, it is a mystery to them. There are some who insist that the speaking in tongues that Pentecostals and charismatics do is just gibberish.

I remember one year, back in the 70's, when I was wondering about that myself. I had heard a lot of people speaking in tongues in prayer rooms, and it did sound like non-sense and gibberish to me. When I spoke in tongues myself, it sounded like non-sense. Could it be that it was just gibberish, and not the real deal that Scripture described? But just because one hears people speaking in tongues and can't understand it, that doesn't mean that it's not a language. God gave me a special experience that helped me understand that. I had made an appointment to meet someone at a small restaurant in the university district (University of Washington). For whatever reason, they got there quite late. I was sitting by myself for about 45 minutes, nursing a Coke and trying to listen to conversations going on around me. It was an open room with 15-20 tables, and it was quite full. Maybe it was the time of day or something, but I suddenly realized that I was having trouble understanding any of the conversations around me, because pretty much all of them were foreign students. They were speaking a number of different languages, and I couldn't understand any of them. It didn't sound structured and logical, like English. In fact most of them just seemed to be repeating similar syllables and sounds. It was like a bunch of gibberish. Ding, ding, ding, ding, ding! A bell went off in my head. This was a restaurant, not a church, and people were just having their regular conversations, just in different languages. And it sounded like gibberish to me,…just like people speaking in tongues in a prayer room. Just because I couldn't understand the words didn't mean that it wasn't a language. Whatever was being said in the small restaurant, or in the church prayer room, was a mystery to me because, while it was being spoken in a language, it wasn't being spoken in a language I knew.

Insight #2 — When one speaks in tongues, he speaks to God.

What this means is that God understands what the message in tongues is. Most people do not know the language spoken in tongues, unless it is in a language they know. Only God knows all languages, so only God knows what every message in tongues is saying. As we look at all Scriptural examples of the gift of speaking in tongues, we can see that at times the tongues is speaking directly to men about God; at other times it is in the form of a prayer, thus speaking directly to God. Regardless of who the tongues is addressed to, God always understands it, so in that sense it is spoken to God.

*I Corinthians 14:4, 5 – One who speaks in a tongue **edifies himself**; but one who prophesies edifies the church. Now **I wish that you all spoke in tongues**, but even more that you would prophesy.*

Jude 1:20 – But you, beloved, building yourselves up on your most holy faith, praying in the Holy Spirit,…

When one speaks in tongues, he edifies himself.

Insight #3 – When one speaks in tongues, he edifies himself.

This is the reason that I cite the most when I encourage people to speak in tongues: it builds you up. I don't know what I am saying when I speak in tongues, but the Holy Spirit provides the utterance, and whatever is being said, does something very good for me: it builds me up. In my times of personal and private prayer, I speak in tongues a lot, and I know that it builds me up. I am thankful that the Holy Spirit provides this tool and gift for me. I need all the building up of myself that I can get; especially the kind of edification that the Holy Spirit does in me.

Now Paul was pointing out to the Corinthians that when they assembled together the goal was for everyone to be built up, not just the individual building himself up and ignoring others around him. The church service is not about self; it is about others. Consequently when I work with prayer teams for the church service, I tell them to get prepared beforehand. Pray, pray in tongues and get your faith and yourself built up, so that in the church service you can pray for others and minister to others in English. That way others are edified (built up).

Do not lose the significant gem: when you speak in tongues, you edify yourself. That's a fantastic tool and gift from the Holy Spirit!

Insight #4 – Paul wishes that all of us spoke in tongues.

He made it clear that in the church service prophecy would benefit everyone hearing, since they could understand it. But he does wish that all spoke in tongues. Many people are willing to allow others to speak in tongues, but they don't want to do it themselves; they don't think they need it or benefit from it. The Apostle Paul wishes that everyone spoke in tongues. He doesn't want tongues spoken in the church service, unless it is interpreted so everyone can understand and get the opportunity to be edified. So when does he want everyone to speak in tongues? Just as he did, he wants you to speak in tongues in your private prayer life. It was good for Paul and it is good for us.

*I Corinthians 14:14, 15 – For if I pray in a tongue, **my spirit prays**, but my mind is unfruitful. What is the outcome then? I will **pray with the spirit** and I will pray with the mind also; I will **sing with the spirit** and I will sing with the mind also.*

Insight #5 – One who speaks in tongues is praying with his spirit.

Sometimes it is hard for me to figure out what's inside of me. I understand that I am made up of body, soul and spirit. The body part is easy: it's all my physical stuff. My soul is made up of my mind, my emotions and my volition (my chooser; my decider). My spirit is the tough part for me to understand and to really connect with. Let's not forget that as a Christian believer I have God inside of me: His Spirit is right there beside my spirit inside of me. But sometimes it's hard for me to sense and connect with my own spirit within. It's also hard, at times, to sense His Holy Spirit within me. I know He's there, but I don't feel him. But there are those rare times when I feel my spirit and I feel His Spirit, and I know I am moving in the spiritual realm.

When I consider the gifts of the Spirit, especially the vocal ones (word of knowledge, word of wisdom, prophecy, tongues, interpretation), I am developing a better understanding. God's Spirit within me puts the gift on my spirit within me. Then my spirit moves to speak the gift through my soul. Now that can be a problem point. For example: the Lord has used me in the gift of prophecy over the last 35 years. I have sometimes made mistakes in ministering the gift. His Spirit puts the prophecy on my spirit; then my mind starts thinking about the content and my emotions start reacting to the message, and before you know it I get some of my thoughts and feelings mixed into the God-given prophecy. If I speak the prophecy with my intellectual and emotional additions, I have diluted God's gift. That's not what God wants to happen. In recent years I have been much better about prophesying, because I work hard to keep my mind and emotions out of it, and just speak what God wants spoken. Now I'm not trying to be humorous here, but I have noticed that the prophecies I minister these days are much shorter than they used to be!

Now the beauty of speaking in tongues is that my mind doesn't understand the message and my emotions don't react to what I don't understand. His Spirit puts the utterance on my spirit, and my spirit speaks it out. I am praying with my spirit when I speak in tongues. This helps me connect with my own spirit. I sense my spirit better and I sense the spiritual realm better. Speaking in tongues helps me better sense, understand and move in the spiritual dimension.

I Corinthians 14:18 – ***I thank God, I speak in tongues more than you all.***

Insight #6 – Paul spoke in tongues more than any of the Corinthian Christians.

Paul was a tongues talker! Remember who we are talking about here. Paul was writing to the Corinthian church, and that church had a lot of tongues talkers. Their church services were out of order because so many people were talking so much in tongues. Yet Paul said he spoke in tongues more than all of them. More than that, he thanked God that he spoke in tongues more than all of them. Yet in the church Paul said he would rather speak five words in the language the Corinthians understood than ten thousand words in tongues, so that the people hearing would be encouraged and built up. So if Paul did not speak tongues in the church service, when did he speak more tongues than all of them? The answer has to be in his private, personal, devotional times of prayer. Jesus taught strongly that private prayer (all alone in your prayer closet) was vital for each Christian and valued and appreciated by the Father. If Paul was speaking in tongues a lot in his private prayer time, it should be obvious that we should do the same, and that it is good for us. Paul was not some emotional, experiential flake. He was an apostle of the Lord Jesus Christ. Let's follow him in speaking in tongues, as He followed Christ.

I Corinthians 14:39 – desire earnestly to prophesy, and ***do not forbid to speak in tongues.***

Insight #7 – Paul commanded that no one forbids others from speaking in tongues.

Paul gave clear instruction to the Corinthian church: come back into balance; seek to abound for the edification of everyone. You are to desire earnestly to prophesy and it will help you come back into balance. Then he concluded with a big but. He did not want them to go out of balance in the other way. So he commanded: don't forbid to speak in tongues. This whole chapter makes me wish for two things: 1-I wish that all the present day Pentecostals would seek to have balance in their services and practices, so that the whole church can be built up. 2-I wish that the non-Pentecostals would seek to have balance in their services and practices, so that the whole church can benefit from the Holy Spirit gift of speaking in tongues.

These seven insights are gems from the Apostle Paul. They are simple and straightforward. Benefit from these gems and be open to speaking in tongues: it's good for you!

Chapter Ten

PRAYING IN THE SPIRIT

A key gift that the Holy Spirit uses to build us up

I Corinthians 14:14, 15 – *For if I pray in a tongue,* ***my spirit prays****, but my mind is unfruitful. What is the outcome then? I will* ***pray with the spirit*** *and I will pray with the mind also; I will* ***sing with the spirit*** *and I will sing with the mind also.*

Pray with the Spirit. Here Paul helps us to understand that when we speak in tongues, we are proclaiming or praying with our spirit. Paul makes the very logical case that when one is speaking in tongues in a church service, it doesn't help the rest of the people in the service, unless they can understand it. And the proper way for them to have the opportunity to understand the message in tongues and agree with it, is if the individual speaking in tongues also follows up with the gift of interpretation of tongues. Obviously the person speaking in tongues doesn't understand what he is saying. But since the gift of tongues is from the Holy Spirit, He understands the message and can give the interpretation to the person speaking the tongues. That's why Paul says, "I will pray with the spirit (message in tongues) and I will pray with the mind also (interpretation of tongues). I will sing with the spirit (a song in tongues) and I will sing with the mind also (interpretation of the tongues in song).

We now exist in the physical realm and the spiritual realm at the same time.

We are quite accustomed to praying in English, and we do it with our mind, the intellectual part of our soul. We are also used to being aware of the physical world all around us. Our physical senses report things to our brain, and our minds interpret the messages from our nervous systems. When we pray in tongues, we do it with our spirit, the spiritual dimension part of our being. It is hard for us to know, grasp, understand, feel, etc., our spirit. Our spirit has spiritual senses, by which we are aware of the spiritual world all around us. Our spiritual senses see, hear and feel the spiritual dimension. Now that's a lot harder for us to do, because it's not what we are used to. All of our life we have used our physical senses to be aware of the physical world around us. So we're really good at that. But we're novices when it comes to using our spiritual senses to be aware of the spiritual world around us. All of our lives we have known and accepted our physical existence in the physical world around us. Well, as Christians we have spiritual existence in the spiritual world around us. That's right: we now exist in the physical realm and the spiritual realm at the same time. We don't just bounce in and out of the spiritual dimension; we exist in it in the same way that we exist in the physical dimension. We have been born again:

John 3:6 – That which is born of the flesh is flesh, and that which is born of the Spirit is spirit.

God has given us the gift of speaking in tongues as a very special gift to help us with our sensing, understanding and walking in the spiritual dimension. The Holy Spirit is inside of us, and, of course, our own spirit is within us. The Holy Spirit gives a tongues message and/or prayer to us by laying it on our spirit. Our mind can't understand it, so we reach inside to embrace the Holy Spirit and "sense" both His presence and the tongues message. Then by faith we speak the message in tongues. The more we do this, the better we get at sensing, understanding and walking in the spiritual dimension. I'm saying all this to help you understand how valuable this gift of speaking in tongues is for our Christian walk. All of us should pray with the spirit more and more. It's why Paul said he thanked God that he spoke in tongues more than all the Corinthian believers.

*Ephesians 6:18 – With all prayer and petition **pray at all times in the Spirit**, and with this in view, be on the alert with all perseverance and petition for all the saints.*

Pray in the Spirit. The Greek work for "Spirit" is not capitalized in the original, but we can conclude it is referring to the Spirit of God, so we capitalize it in the English. When the translation is made into English, the translator has to look at all the context and decide whether it is talking about a human spirit or the Holy Spirit. Here in Ephesians Paul had just discussed the elements of spiritual dimension warfare and pointed directly at the sword of the Spirit, the word of God. Then he moves into instruction for prayer and alertness: pray at all times in the Spirit. Throw yourself into spiritual awareness, intercession and warfare. Reach inside to apprehend His Spirit: take hold of Him, embrace Him. In that closeness to the Holy Spirit, your prayer, whether in English or in tongues from Him, is right in the center of God, and you can press into praying for everyone as a vigilant warrior of the

Lord Jesus Christ. This kind of praying in the Spirit is our powerful weapon and battle plan for the spiritual dimension! Don't try to find some light saber or mind power. Just grab onto the Spirit and pray for everyone and everything: that's the battle plan and the secret weapon. Praying in the Spirit certainly includes prayer in tongues, but it also means any prayer we pray that comes from our position in this mutual embrace with the Holy Spirit. He's hugging you, you're hugging Him and that's close communion in prayer!

The hollow clunk of a little boy's skull hitting the tile floor very hard!

Recently my daughter was working in the kitchen with her three children. Her two daughters (Age 10 and 12) enjoy helping her with cooking and baking. Her two-year old boy loves to be in the room with them, and usually wants to eat whatever they are working on. On this particular day the little boy got quite active climbing on things while the three ladies were a bit distracted by the food preparation. Suddenly all three of them heard a dreaded sound: the hollow clunk of a little boy's skull hitting the tile floor very hard! A parent can tell when the accident and sound is really serious...maybe critical. My daughter grabbed up her little boy and also grabbed hold of the Holy Spirit within her. Prayer in tongues came flowing out of her mouth in an intense gush of communication. The result? The little guy was fine and resumed his energetic activities. My daughter shared this with me; she was convinced the Holy Spirit helped her with intercessory

PRAYING IN THE SPIRIT

prayer and the little guy was healed by the Lord Jesus Christ on the spot. Pray in the Spirit because it works!

Jude 20 – But you, beloved, ***building yourselves up on your most holy faith, praying in the Holy Spirit,*** *keep yourselves in the love of God,…*

I Corinthians 14:4 – One who speaks in a tongue ***edifies himself;****…*

Pray to build yourself up (praying in tongues, praying in the Holy Spirit). This Greek word is straightforward: to edify, to build up. An edifice is a fancy word for a really fancy building (like a cathedral or capitol building). Edify means to build up. Jesus Christ taught His disciples that their most important prayers should be in private, alone in their prayer closet. In fact that's the context for Him giving them the Lord's Prayer. And the Scriptures do teach us that praying in tongues builds us up. I accept that by faith, and, make it a part of my prayer life for strengthening. I have trained prayer team members to pray for other people who come forward after the service for special prayer. I encourage the team members to pray privately or in small groups before the service, so that they are ready to pray the prayer of faith for whoever needs it. The time for praying in tongues is before the service, building yourself up in your faith, so that you are an encouragement and faith leader as you pray for others. But when you are there after the service praying for someone else, you need to be praying in English, not tongues, so that they can understand your prayer and be lifted up and encouraged in their faith and life.

Romans 8:26 – In the same way the Spirit also helps our weaknesses; for we do not know how to pray as we should, but the Spirit Himself intercedes for us with groanings ***too deep for words;***

Romans 8:34 – ...Christ Jesus is He who died, yes, rather who was raised, who is at the right hand of God, who also intercedes for us.

Holy Spirit intercessory prayer. The intercession that the Holy Spirit makes for us is tremendous. This is the only place that this particular Greek word is used, and it could be translated "super-intercession" or "higher level intercession." We know from other Scripture that Jesus Christ is doing special intercession for us. Jesus is in the authority position at the right hand of the Father, eager and ready to intercede for us. The Holy Spirit knows what needs to be prayed on our behalf, so He expresses it, and super-super-intercession happens on our behalf! How awesome is that?

Having said that, however, I have to point out something to my Pentecostal brethren. Many people have told me that this groaning super-intercession that the Holy Spirit does for us is speaking in tongues. It is not. The Greek words translated "too deep for words," literally means "cannot be uttered." It is a fantastic intercession, and I am so thankful for this work of the Holy Spirit; but it is not speaking in tongues. Don't short change yourself. As you pray, let the Holy Spirit go deep, really deep, and intercede for you with groanings that are so deep they are not even being uttered.

Be set free to pray in all the ways that you can, including praying in tongues. Pray with your spirit; pray in the Spirit. Pray to build yourself up, so that you can build up and encourage others, and ultimately bring more people to the Lord. The Lord's will is that all should come to repentance, and our ultimate goal is always His will, His kingdom and His righteousness. No Christian stands alone to seek benefits for himself alone. Every Christian wants to bring encouragement and benefit to others; to his fellow Christians, to those non-Christians who are seeking the truth, and to all people, even if they aren't interested in the Lord. In the last days before Jesus returns, the Holy Spirit will draw people to the church. These people will want to be taught the ways of the Lord, and how to walk in them. We are responsible to be all that we can be and do all that we can do, to teach them the Lord's ways. Let the Holy Spirit and His gift of speaking in tongues be part of your equipment in ministering to others!

Chapter Eleven

IS THIS GIFT FOR YOU?

It was good for Paul, but is it good enough for you?

A Christian does not have to speak in tongues. Every Christian is saved by having faith in the saving grace of Jesus Christ. We are the righteousness of God in Him, and no gift of the Holy Spirit is required for us to be saved. Having said that, the Bible presents a strong case for the benefits and advantages that speaking in tongues can bring to every individual Christian.

- Speaking in tongues does give self-edification. The Christian who speaks in tongues builds himself up. When one speaks in tongues, he edifies himself.

- Speaking in tongues speaks mysteries to God. The Christian who speaks in tongues does not understand what he is saying. But the Holy Spirit provides the content and God does understand it. That's a good thing. When one speaks in tongues, he speaks mysteries to God.

- Paul spoke in tongues a lot (but not in the church services). In everything Paul did in his walk with the Lord, we want to emulate him. We often say, "Follow

Paul as he followed Jesus." He was a phenomenal apostle of the Lord Jesus Christ and we should follow him in the practice of speaking in tongues. Paul spoke in tongues more than any of the Corinthian Christians, but he did it decently and in order when he was in church services; and he did it in his private, devotional communication with Jesus.

Paul wishes that all of us would speak in tongues.

- Paul thought that all Christians should speak in tongues. He wanted all Christians to speak in tongues (but not in the church services). For the many Christians who have avoided speaking in tongues because some have abused it by being selfish or out of order, take note of Paul's approach. He didn't tell anyone to stop speaking in tongues, but he did give instruction so that the selfish use of the gift could be corrected, and then ministry of the gifts of the Spirit would be decent and in order in the church services. Paul wishes that all of us would speak in tongues.

- Speaking in tongues is your spirit praying in the Spirit. The Holy Spirit provides the message in tongues and deposits it on your spirit. Then you speak the tongues with your spirit. So you are not just making the tongues up with your mind, or remembering certain tongue phrases with your mind and speaking them. Each time you speak in tongues it is your spirit praying the message in tongues that the Holy Spirit has laid upon your spirit. Let it be of the Holy Spirit, and never pollute it with your mind or emotions.

Paul commanded that no one should forbid others from speaking in tongues.

- Speaking in tongues is never to be forbidden. Paul commanded that no one should forbid others from speaking in tongues. While no one should be pressured to speak in tongues, no one should forbid tongues.

- Speaking in tongues in the church service is beneficial if it is accompanied by interpretation of tongues. That's why both are listed among the gifts of the Spirit in I Corinthians 12. The tongues may be a message from God to His people that brings encouragement, edification and comfort. It may also be a prayer addressed to God; an extraordinary and beautiful prayer, because the Spirit of God Himself is actually framing the right prayer for the moment, that correctly addresses the situation to God.

- Speaking in tongues is most often for the individual Christian, between himself and God. It is personal, private, devotional and individualized. It is in this private prayer practice that Paul could say he spoke in tongues more than all the Corinthian Christians.

Speaking in tongues; do it a lot. It's good for you!

Part Three

Gifts of the Spirit - For Touching God's People

"Pursue love, yet desire earnestly spiritual gifts,"

I Corinthians 14:1

Chapter Twelve

HOLY SPIRIT MINISTRY GIFTS

Regular people touching regular people
with God's special help

I Corinthians 12:4-11 – Now there are varieties of gifts, but the same Spirit. And there are varieties of ministries, and the same Lord. There are varieties of effects, but the same God who works all things in all persons. But to each one is given the manifestation of the Spirit for the common good. For to one is given the word of wisdom through the Spirit, and to another the word of knowledge according to the same Spirit; to another faith by the same Spirit, and to another gifts of healing by the one Spirit, and to another the effecting of miracles, and to another prophecy, and to another the distinguishing of spirits, to another various kinds of tongues, and to another the interpretation of tongues. But one and the same Spirit works all these things, distributing to each one individually just as He wills.

The gifts of the Spirit have been talked about and practiced in the church for almost 2,000 years. The nine gifts listed in I Corinthians 12:6-8 are the most well known: word of wisdom, word of knowledge, faith, gifts of healing, effecting of miracles, prophecy, distinguishing of spirits, tongues, interpretation of tongues. They are most often referred to as the gifts of the Spirit and their use by Christians, especially in church services, is well presented by Paul in I Corinthians chapters 12-14. In this Holy Ghost primer I want to cover five of these gifts in particular because it is valuable and vital for every loving Christian to know what these gifts are, and how they are to be used in the best possible way for His church.

But these are not the only gifts of the Spirit. Here's a quick presentation of many Holy Spirit gifts that show the broad and encompassing way the Holy Spirit wants to minister through His people. It's the way that regular people can touch regular people with God's special help. Consider these Scriptures:

I Corinthians 12:28-31 – And God has appointed in the church, first apostles, second prophets, third teachers, then miracles, then gifts of healings, helps, administrations, various kinds of tongues. All are not apostles, are they? All are not prophets, are they? All are not teachers, are they? All are not workers of miracles, are they? All do not have gifts of healings, do they? All do not speak with tongues, do they? All do not interpret, do they? But earnestly desire the greater gifts.

Nine gifts are listed; four of them were mentioned in our previous Scripture but five are different: apostles, prophets, teachers, helps and administrations. These gifts are appointed by God in the church.

Acts 2:17, 18 – 'AND IT SHALL BE IN THE LAST DAYS,' God *says*, 'THAT I WILL POUR FORTH OF MY SPIRIT ON ALL MANKIND; AND YOUR SONS AND YOUR DAUGHTERS SHALL PROPHESY, AND YOUR YOUNG MEN SHALL SEE VISIONS, AND YOUR OLD MEN SHALL DREAM DREAMS; EVEN ON MY BONDSLAVES, BOTH MEN AND WOMEN, I WILL IN THOSE DAYS POUR FORTH OF MY SPIRIT *and they shall prophesy.*

Three gifts are listed: prophecies, visions, and dreams. These gifts are poured forth by God's Spirit on all Christian men and women, young and old.

Romans 12:6-8 – Since we have gifts that differ according to the grace given to us, each of us is to exercise them accordingly: if prophecy, according to the proportion of his faith; if service, in his serving; or he who teaches, in his teaching; or he who exhorts, in his exhortation; he who gives, with liberality; he who leads, with diligence; he who shows mercy, with cheerfulness.

Seven gifts are listed; six of them are different from the first list in I Corinthians chapter twelve: serving, teaching, exhortation, giving, leading, showing mercy. These gifts are given by grace to individual Christians.

Ephesians 4:11, 12 – And he gave some as apostles, and some as prophets, and some as evangelists, and some as pastors and teachers, for the equipping of the saints for the work of service, to the building up of the body of Christ;

Five gifts are listed; two different from the previous four Scriptures: evangelists and pastors. These are gifts God gave to men, for the purpose of equipping Christians for ministry.

I Peter 4:10, 11 – As each one has received a special gift, employ it in serving one another as good stewards of the manifold grace of God. Whoever speaks, is to do so as one who is speaking the utterances of God; whoever serves is to do so as one who is serving by the strength which God supplies; so that in all things God may be glorified through Jesus Christ, to whom belongs the glory and dominion forever and ever. Amen.

Two gifts are listed; one different from the previous lists: speaking. These are gifts given by God's varied grace

Exodus 31:1-5 – Now the LORD spoke to Moses, saying, "See, I have called by name Bezalel, the son of Uri, the son of Hur, of the tribe of

Judah. I have filled him with the Spirit of God in wisdom, in understanding, in knowledge, and in all kinds of craftsmanship, to make artistic designs for work in gold, in silver, and in bronze, and in the cutting of stones for settings, and in the carving of wood, that he may work in all kinds of craftsmanship.

> **Filled with the Spirit of God in wisdom, understanding and knowledge of all kinds of craftsmanship!**

The gift of craftsmanship is thoroughly described. Filled with the Spirit of God in wisdom, understanding and knowledge of all kinds of craftsmanship! This is a gift of skill, given by God to the individual Bezalel. It was to meet the need of the moment for the building of the tabernacle, and God accomplished the giving of the gift by filling him with His Spirit.

There are also ministry gifts in the area of music identified in several Scriptures, such as prophetic song and selah, from both the Old and New Testament.

Here are some gifts and groupings (by no means all inclusive) that God had identified for us in His Word. Many lists and groupings have been used to teach about the gifts, and there are other Holy Spirit ministry gifts besides these ones. Any particular thing that God has you doing on a regular basis can be a ministry gift, if you have given it up to God, and He has picked it up and given it back to you. He has touched it, and it is thereby divine….supernatural….a ministry gift from the Spirit.

HOLY SPIRIT MINISTRY GIFTS

Leading Gifts
teaching
exhortation
leading
administration
preaching

Musical Gifts
new song
prophetic song
tongues in song
selah
musician gifted by God

Office Gifts
apostle
prophet
evangelist
pastor
teacher

Serving Gifts
helps
serving
giving
showing mercy

Miracle Gifts
gift of faith
healings
miracles
discerning of spirits

Verbal Gifts
word of knowledge
word of wisdom
prophecy
speaking in tongues
interpretation of tongues
dreams and visions
gift of speaking

Gift of Craftsmanship

Regular people touching regular people with God's special help.

I've listed thirty-one gifts here, and of course, God has many more. Some of the gifts seem like something only God could do, while others appear to be something human effort could accomplish. But they all are supernatural if God has touched them! I want all of us to see that Holy Spirit ministry gifts are given to every one of us. This is about regular people touching regular people with God's special help.

I want us to look at five gifts in particular, but before we do that, I want to outline nine fundamental operational truths. You will find them in the previous Scriptures we have referenced about the many gifts, but I also want to add these additional Scriptures for you to review, as they help us see the simple, yet profound fundamental truths that set us on the path of successfully using the ministry gifts of the Spirit.

I Corinthians 13:1-8 – If I speak with the tongues of men and of angels, (referring to the gift of tongues) *but do not have love, I have become a noisy gong or a clanging cymbal. If I have the gift of prophecy, and know all mysteries and all knowledge* (referring to the word of wisdom and the word of knowledge) *and if I have all faith, so as to remove mountains, but do not have love, I am nothing. And if I give all my possessions to feed the poor, and if I surrender my body to be burned, but do not have love, it profits me nothing. Love is patient, love is kind and is not jealous; love does not brag and is not arrogant, does not act unbecomingly; it does not seek its own, is not provoked, does not take into account a wrong suffered, does not rejoice in unrighteousness, but rejoices with the truth; bears all things, believes all things, hopes all things, endures all things. Love never fails, but if there are gifts of prophecy, they will be done away; if there are tongues, they will cease, if there is knowledge, it will be done away.*

I Corinthians 14:1 – Pursue love, yet desire earnestly spiritual gifts, but especially that you may prophesy.

HOLY SPIRIT MINISTRY GIFTS

I Corinthians 14:12 – So also you, since you are zealous of spiritual gifts, seek to abound for the edification of the church.

Before you consider the fundamental truths, and moving forward into the proper, successful exercising of the ministry gifts of the Holy Spirit, please listen to this. When gifts are ministered, mistakes sometimes happen. God does not make mistakes, so...we Christians must be making the mistakes. That's what we want to avoid. If you don't remember anything remember this:

Get your soul straight in ministering your gifts!

Get your soul straight in ministering your gifts!

Get your thinking straight, get your desires straight and get your feelings straight!

All for Him, none for you, and He will accomplish the miraculous through you!

1. **Every Christian receives a special ministry gift(s). I Peter 4:10, 11.** Christians who already minister the gifts of the Spirit know this, but I am addressing the many Christians who don't minister the gifts. The church needs you; the body of Christ needs your ministry; the Lord wants to use you in His gifts! When you look around a typical Sunday morning service, you will see many observers. According to God's Word every Christian has been given special ministry gifts.

That means that God wants every Christian to be a participant, not an observer.

2. **There is a variety of gifts, ministries and effects. I Corinthians 12:4-6.** Since God is the gift giver, we can all see that He would provide a variety. But we Christians sometimes get bogged down in trying to define the correct pattern, and have everyone do it that way. In other words we go beyond defining the gift and want to dictate the course, channel and pattern. In doing that we sometimes thwart what the Holy Spirit is trying to accomplish. Also, the ministering of many gifts brings about many results and effects. If we don't like those results, we try to limit gifts and ministries to avoid getting those results again. But God knows that this whole area of ministry gifts has variety, variety, variety! So we need to lighten up, ease off, stop gripping so hard, and let God have His way. We can do that and still have decency and order in the church.

3. **Everyone doesn't exercise the same gift. I Corinthians 12:28-30.** For whatever reason, humans like to look alike, act alike and be alike. In order to flock together, we dress ourselves with the same feathers. This can happen in a church: one or two particular gifts (tongues, for instance) look good to everyone, and so almost everyone wants that gift. This creates imbalance in the congregation, just as was the case in the city of Corinth. So each one of us needs to discover and use the gifts that are unique to our individual self. Don't be a mimic; when it comes to the gifts of the Spirit, you are an original. And don't be caught up in admiring certain "sparkly," "pizazzy" gifts. Every Christian and every gift is equally special!

4. **The gifts differ according to the grace given to us. Romans 12:6.** God gives each one of us, individually, the grace to minister our gifts. The grace is His favor and empowering to successfully exercise our gifts. God gives this grace in different ways and amounts. He judges the situation, our own level of spiritual wisdom and knowledge, and our position with regard to covering and authority, and then He gives us the appropriate grace to minister. Wow! That's a huge mouthful, but accept it in a simple way: God will give you the grace needed to minister the right thing at the right time, and it will work out right!

5. **The gifts are given according to the will of the Spirit. I Corinthians 12:11.** It goes without saying that we have our own likes, wants and desires, but it is the will of the Holy Spirit that determines the giving of His gifts. I remember my first couple of years at Bible College. My goal was to be an evangelist; fiery preaching with miracle services, as I traveled the nation. But about two years into the training process, I began to realize that God wanted me to be a pastor; one who systematically taught the Word of God, and worked with people over years, as they grew and developed. I had to set aside my own aspirations and desires, and submit to what God wanted me to be. The gifts are given according to the will of the Holy Spirit, not according to our wants and desires. He decides who is given which gifts at which times. Each of us needs to come to the point where our greatest desire is to do what God wants us to do, where He wants it done and when He wants it done. When we are in that frame of mind, we can exercise ministry gifts of the Spirit according to what He wants.

6. **The gifts are for the common good. I Corinthians 12:7.** I see two things happen that contradict the "common good" goal. First there are Christians who like the fame and fortune that can come to them personally when they exercise the gifts. It feeds their own ego and pride. The second thing is more subtle: some Christians enjoy the strengthening that can come from certain gifts. For example the gift of tongues does build up the individual speaking. That should be an encouraged practice for all of us. But for some they stop at that point, enjoying what the gift does for them, but not moving on to the real purpose of the gifts. The good that the ministry gifts of the Spirit can do is meant for "the common," that is, for everyone; not just for the individual ministering the gifts.

7. **The gifts are for serving one another. I Peter 4:10.** I want to cut through all the pretty words and semantics. In the latter part of the 20th century we have come to use the words "minister" and "ministry" as a noble description of what we do. They are really just words to mean "serve" and "service." When we look a little harder, the Greek words really are describing what a slave does. Do you remember when Jesus washed the feet of His disciples? "You also ought to wash one another's feet." When we exercise the gifts of the Spirit we are slaves serving one another. The ministry gifts of the Spirit are for serving one another.

8. **The excellent way to exercise the gifts is in love. I Corinthians 12:31, 13:1-8.** The love chapter says it all. If we don't exercise the ministry gifts of the Holy Spirit in love, we are nothing, and we make nothing of the gifts.

9. **We should earnestly desire the greater gifts. I Corinthians 12:31; 14:1; 14:12.** Some people who read I Corinthians chapters 12-14 conclude that prophecy is one of the greater gifts for all of us to desire. That's not accurate. Looking carefully at the church in Corinth, and how they practiced the different gifts of the Spirit, it is obvious that they were out of balance toward the gift of tongues, and needed to have gifts that were understandable and would build up everyone, in order to come back into balance. For them the gift of prophecy was the greater gift to be earnestly desired, so that their church could come back into balance. That's what we all need to earnestly desire. The gifts that will keep our church balanced and edified are the "greater gifts" that we are to earnestly desire.

These are nine fundamental truths that help us construct the perfect foundation upon which to exercise the ministry gifts of the Holy Spirit. Now let's look at five of these specific gifts.

Chapter Thirteen

WORD OF WISDOM AND WORD OF KNOWLEDGE

Regular people speaking divine revelations of wisdom and knowledge to regular people

Word of Knowledge (Greek – utterance of knowledge). This gift is a supernatural utterance from the Holy Spirit that reveals certain facts in the mind of God, which we otherwise would not know. This gift reveals facts. It answers the questions: What's happening? What's going on?

People sometimes don't understand what's happening in their lives. They look for someone to tell them what's going on. As a pastor I have had many people over the years come to me for help because they don't understand the circumstances of their life. "Pastor, what's going on? What's happening? Can you help me?" In the altar times at the end of our church services, my wife and I have the privilege of praying for anyone who comes forward for prayer. Often they want to take considerable time to tell us what's going on with their lives. I know that the reason they are taking so long to fill us in on details is because they are hoping that we can answer the question: "What's happening to us?" Sometimes I can understand what's happening to them because I have more life knowledge and experience than they do, so I impart that knowledge to them. But there are other times when I really don't know what's happening. I can't figure it out. Thankfully God does not abandon His children in these situations. He knows everything and He has the answer to their question. That's when I am so thankful for the word of knowledge from the Holy Spirit. He often gives us a word of knowledge and when we share it with them, it really helps!

Word of Wisdom (Greek – utterance of wisdom). This gift is a supernatural utterance from the Holy Spirit that tells how to apply knowledge, supernatural or otherwise. While knowledge is awareness of facts, wisdom is the proper application of knowledge in a given situation. This gift gives direction. It answers the question: What should I do?

People are often looking for advice. As a pastor I have had hundreds of people over the years seeking advice and counsel. My wife and I work together regularly as a prayer team for people who come to the altar. Whether it's a brother or sister asking for prayer, or congregational members asking for advice or counsel, it most often boils down to this question: "What should I do?" I will tell you that sometimes I know what someone should do, and I share that. But there are times when I am at a loss. Sometimes it is because I don't have all the facts. Sometimes I have all the facts and I still don't have a clue as to what should be done! I have no idea what they should do. That's when I am so thankful for the word of wisdom from the Holy Spirit.

We will look at the word of knowledge and the word of wisdom together because I have personally seen them work hand in hand, and be ministered together. Remember the questions Christians most often have: "What's going on?"

WORD OF WISDOM AND WORD OF KNOWLEDGE

"What's happening?" "What should I do?" It's almost automatic that once you discover what's going on, then you want to know what to do.

I can remember church prayer times, from the time I was seven years old, going with my mother to Pentecostal church services. Whether it was a regular Sunday service with hundreds of people, or a smaller group meeting of a dozen or less, there was always opportunity given for people to be prayed for. The approach always seemed the same: the group leader would ask if anyone had a prayer request. Many people would avail themselves of the opportunity to be prayed for, and they would voice a specific request: "I need to get a job;" "My grandmother fell and broke her hip;" "My son has run away from home;" "I have a big test tomorrow;" "I haven't heard back from my job interview;" "Our cat is lost;" "I've been diagnosed with cancer;" and so on. It was always a good time, when we would gather around someone, usually laying hands on them and pouring out our hearts in agreement, praying for the Lord to help. It was always good to be with a bunch of God's people praying their hearts out for someone's special need.

But one thing puzzled me as a child. There was always at least one person who would say, "Unspoken request." It didn't matter whether it was the Sunday night service, Tuesday night prayer meeting, young people's meeting (CA's), women's gathering (WMC's) (yes; Mom would sometimes take us kids along to the women's meeting); or even a revival meeting; one or more people would always have an "unspoken request." I also remember that it was often the same people who had the "unspoken requests." Now here's how my young mind worked: what do you mean, an unspoken request? How can anyone pray for you if you don't say the request? I would listen to how people would pray for the "unspoken request," and the prayers seemed so vague and indefinite. Unspoken requests made no sense to me at all. As I grew older I came to realize two things: 1-there were people who had problems that were too personal to speak out loud, and it was better not to share details; 2-there were people who were dramatic and used "unspoken request" as an attention getter.

> **Come together, come into agreement, come into unity – that's the formula.**

I share my "unspoken request" memories to bring attention to the reality that we like to know what's going on so we can pray with knowledge. But as adults we need to understand that discretion is important in any relationship. All you have to do is follow Facebook to realize that many people have lost all idea of what not to share. There really are legitimate times when it is better that we don't know all the details of a situation with one of our Christian brothers or sisters. But let's be honest: we really want to know as much as we can, so that we know how to pray and we can give practical, godly advice. If our motive is to find out juicy details so we can judge or gossip, that is extremely wrong, and God does not look on it kindly when we mistreat one of His children. But knowing how to pray and what good advice to give is very important, and we should be able to do that for one another. So how do we handle the details of our life when we come together with other Christian brothers and sisters? Our goal is to be in unity just as our Lord Jesus Christ wants us to be. We are responsible to come together and do our best to come into agreement: come together, come into agreement, come into unity – that's the formula. That is our path to godly unity. But I do recommend that all of us be circumspect and discrete. If you have tough stuff to share, develop a good, confidential relationship with one or two others, whom you can trust to be discrete and maintain your confidence. A lot of the time that can be your pastor. And if a brother or sister shares a confidence with you, be discrete and honorable. Love covers a multitude of sins (I Peter 4:8).

Back to our desire to find out as many details as possible, so that we know how to pray and so that we can give godly advice. The truth is that there are times when we don't get to know things. How do we solve this dilemma? Easy! God knows everything and knows the best "Godly" advice. We can depend upon Holy Spirit ministry gifts to meet the need. Isn't it great that we aren't dependent upon human knowledge and wisdom to successfully minister? We have the knowledge and wisdom of God at our disposal, whenever He sees that we need it. This concept applies equally to the word of knowledge and the word of wisdom.

Let's look at some specific examples of how the word of knowledge works. Recently a young married couple came forward after a church service and asked my wife and I to pray for them. The wife shared that their relationship with her husband's family was falling apart, and needed to be healed and restored. The husband had done something wrong that affected other members of the family. He knew he had done wrong, had apologized to the family and was trying to make amends. But the family, especially his father, was not forgiving him or wanting to have anything to do with him. The wife had tried to talk with his dad, but had been rudely shut down. They wanted prayer for God's help and guidance in what to do. At this point the Lord gave me a word of knowledge: the wife was taking the burden of relationship restoration on herself, and she needed to step back, take her hands off the situation, and let her husband take the lead communicating with his family. Now if you look at that word from God, you can see there is both knowledge ("what's going on?") and wisdom ("what should we do?") in the revelation. I spoke to her, saying that God had impressed upon me that she was trying to take the whole responsibility and burden for the situation on herself. She tearfully agreed that she was doing that. I could tell that this was a heavy emotional burden for her. I then told them that God had impressed upon me that she needed to let go of the situation, and let her husband take care of communicating with his family members. We all agreed together in prayer, asking for the blessing of the Lord on the husband's communications with his family. This was the answer they needed and the guidance we needed in knowing how to pray.

Many years ago I was the pastor of a small church in Washington. A young man who was active in the gay life style had come to our church, asking for help. He was unhappy, felt trapped and wanted to be free. He accepted Jesus Christ as his Savior, and started the process of living the new life of a born again believer. I remember I was attending a conference somewhere in Oregon, and was on the phone having a conversation with one of the elders of our church. He mentioned that he had not recently seen the young man and asked if I knew how he was doing. He had developed a close, discipling relationship with him. Suddenly I received a word of knowledge from the Lord. God told me that the young man was sleeping with one of the divorced women in the congregation. On my own I did not have one thought or inkling of such a thing. But God knew that as church leaders we needed to know that and take action. Still on the phone call, I told the elder what God had just told me, and instructed him to go to the home and take redemptive and decisive action to help the young man and woman recover from the sinful situation. I want to add that both the young man and divorced woman were helped in conviction, repentance and situational change, and continued in the congregation, serving the Lord. Praise God for His loving intervention!

Back in the early 70's, while I was attending Bible College in Kirkland, WA, my wife and I participated in a Kathryn Kuhlman Crusade in Seattle. We had never met her, but were very aware of her reputation as a faith healer. We were part of the Crusade Choir, and also altar workers. We had the privilege of watching the main service for several nights in a row. Many people received miraculous healings, including blind people seeing! But Kathryn did not lay hands on people for them to receive healing. It was not what you sometimes see these days on Christian T.V., where a certain leader lays hands on people and they get healed. It was dramatic: she wore long, flowing, modest gowns, and fans were strategically placed; maybe to keep her cool, or maybe to keep her gown flowing and moving. The crusade was handled very professionally and the staging for each evening brought everyone's focus upon Kathryn, and that was crucial, because it was the words of knowledge that she spoke that revealed the supernatural healings and brought many to Christ. At any rate she would say: "I don't heal anyone. I don't lay hands on people to get them healed. Please do not come up to be prayed for, unless you are specifically called out." Then she would call out people by the section they were sitting in, and the infirmity they needed healing for. "Someone in the lower right section has prostate cancer and God wants to heal them now. Come forward." If no one responded, then she would zero in, row by row until the person was identified. It was uncanny, miraculous and divine. God would give her words of knowledge, one right after another, and she would speak them until someone responded to the description. She would ask them to come forward and give testimony of their healing. Sometimes she would say, "God is healing you now." Other times she would say, "Come forward and claim your healing." It was wonderful as person after person was healed and would come forward to testify of God's healing power. She would conclude each crusade night with an invitation for people to come forward and accept Jesus Christ as their Savior and Lord. Many were saved during her crusade, and many were divinely healed. This was a phenomenal manifestation of the word of knowledge. It was real, and we saw real healings! I appreciated how she gave the glory to God, and used the circumstance of divine healing as an evangelistic outreach, so that more people accepted Jesus Christ.

In another situation I was on vacation with my family, and was approached in Pensacola by a man we had met a year before. I want you to know that one of the things I pray about for our vacation times is that the Lord would use us in prophetic gifts to help people we come across: friends, acquaintances or strangers. I have decided that I'm not going to take vacation from ministering to people. What's unique here is that the situation was reversed. This gentleman came up to me and said that the Lord had put a word on his heart for me, and asked if he could share it. I readily agreed, and he told me that God was going to bring a new person into my life to minister to; and that the situation would get difficult, but I was to have patience, not give up on them, hang in there, and everything would work out. The Holy Spirit had given him this word for me, and he was faithful to carefully minister it to me. That happened about six weeks ago. There is someone new that has come into our lives, and we are watching carefully and ministering as we can. I think it is wonderful that this man had the courage to do what he believed the Lord had told him to do. The thing that stuck with me is that I would need to stick in there when some tough things came up. That's

WORD OF WISDOM AND WORD OF KNOWLEDGE

a good forewarning to have. As a 65-year old who has ministered to a lot of people over a lot of years, I do sometimes get impatient with people I minister to, if they aren't doing what they should do. This forewarning will help me hang in there and not give up on somebody.

> But sometimes people aren't hearing so well,
> or listening carefully when God speaks to them.

There are times that God gives a word to someone else for you. Now some people think that God would just speak to a person directly, instead of going through someone else. But sometimes people aren't hearing so well, or listening carefully when God speaks to them. It gets our attention when someone else is given the word for us.

Please note the language, approach and presentation that were used in these examples of the word of knowledge and word of wisdom. "God impressed upon me…" "The Lord put a word on my heart for you. Can I share it?" These are careful, humble words and approaches.

- The word of knowledge and the word of wisdom are truly supernatural, in that individuals don't make them up, or draw from their own experience, and we are to speak the words in such a way that it is clear it is from God. I don't think it is right if we don't acknowledge that it is from God. If God gives me a word of knowledge or wisdom, and I say, "I think this is what is going on, and you should do this," that may make me sound wise, but it takes away the divine impact that God desires. Let's carefully acknowledge the hand of the Holy Spirit.

- But we must be careful that our words or presentation don't come off as pompous, arrogant or dominating. Don't say: "This is God's word," or "Thus saith the Lord," or "I am used by God and you need to heed these words," or "I am a prophet. Listen to me!" When we minister these words to people, we don't want them to feel compelled or forced to accept something or do something.

- We should present the word in such a way that people can consider it. First and foremost, they should look to the Holy Spirit within them for a confirmation or a check. Is this right? Is this wrong? Then they should consult their own pastor/spiritual leader for confirmation or check. Is this right? Is this wrong? When I minister verbal gifts of the Spirit, I always suggest that people use this pattern of confirmation or check.

One more thing: when we are given a word of knowledge or a word of wisdom, we are to speak it. It's not just for our own personal knowledge. God doesn't deal in gossip. We don't hold it inside; instead we look for the correct timing and circumstance in which to speak it. Most of the time it can be spoken one-on-one (or couple-on-couple). There are times that it is better if you ask an elder or a pastor to be there when you speak. If a word is to be spoken in front of a large group or congregation, real caution must be used with discretion and kindness. Remember love is to cover a multitude of sins.

Chapter Fourteen

GIFTS OF HEALING

God supernaturally healing people through regular people

Gifts of healings (Greek-gifts of cures; healings) – This gift is the supernatural intervention of God through a human instrument, to restore health. The Holy Spirit equips a person with this gift to heal people of diseases or infirmities.

We see several examples of this gift of healing in the book of Acts, such as Peter speaking healing to the lame man at the Beautiful Gate in Jerusalem. There is one Scripture from Romans that has helped me see the obvious and evident role of the Holy Spirit in healing.

Romans 8:11 – But if the Spirit of Him who raised Jesus from the dead dwells in you, He who raised Christ Jesus from the dead will also give life to your mortal bodies through His Spirit who dwells in you.

But nothing we do as a Christian can get us into the Spirit.

In Romans chapter eight, Paul expresses the beauty and wonder of being Christians. Because we have accepted Jesus Christ as Savior and Lord, we live according to the Spirit, we set our mind on the things of the Spirit and we live according to the Spirit. Because the Spirit of Christ dwells in us, we are in the Spirit. We develop all kinds of ideas and methods to help us get into the Spirit. We read the Word, we pray fervently, we clear our mind of all thoughts about this world; these are all good things for us to do. But nothing we do as a Christian can get us into the Spirit. Why do I say that? It's because we are already in the Spirit because the Holy Spirit dwells in us. All those things we do to try to get in the Spirit are very good to help us focus on the Spirit within us. All these things that we do affect us: we are turning on our switch of awareness. If we simply realize the Holy Spirit is inside of us, then we are also instantly aware that we are in Him.

Romans 8:9 – However, you are not in the flesh but in the Spirit, if indeed the Spirit of God dwells in you.

Here's what I know from God's Word: Because we have accepted Jesus Christ, the Holy Spirit dwells in us; God dwells in us. The Holy Spirit within us gives life to our mortal bodies. The Greek words here literally mean "makes our physical bodies come to life." It is not just talking about coming to life after we have died. It is talking about our physical bodies being given living energy by the Holy Spirit. Now isn't that what divine healing is all about? For Christians, the Holy Spirit within us is the source of all healing. But what about non-Christians? It is the same Spirit who can heal any person, and every divine healing is an opportunity for others to see the power of God and come to the Lord Jesus Christ.

It is no accident that the wording for this gift consists of two plural words: gifts of healings. The <u>gifts are multiple</u> in the way that healing can take place: through prayer, through words of knowledge, through faith, and so on. I have seen and been a part of divine healings over the years, and there are certainly many different approaches and methods that God uses. The <u>healings are multiple</u> in that healing does not just refer to physical healing. Just as there is healing for the body, there is also healing for the soul and healing for the spirit. Every part of our being requires healing at times.

I regret to say that divine healing has been portrayed to the church in many wild, crazy and phony ways. It is true that there have been fake "faith healers" over the years, who are and have been an embarrassment to the church and a sorrow to the Lord. For every legitimate miraculous gift of God, Satan brings along false and phony forms to mislead people and discredit the church. It is for this reason that many Christians have disavowed the gifts of the Spirit. They don't want to be associated in any way, shape or form with phony and false claims. Leaders have staged phony healings; others have presented themselves as special faith healers. They dramatically lay hands on people; they forcefully push on people's heads or shoulders, so that they fall (supposedly slain in the Spirit). They promise that the people in their TV viewing audience will receive healings, if they give certain offerings by faith. They claim to have healing hands, or they have gold dust on their hands, in order to touch people and bestow healing. Some of the people doing this are sorely misguided Christians. I have seen certain Christian leaders abuse this area of divine healing, but eventually repent and change. I do believe it is a serious sin of pride that we see when these "healing shows" are staged. Others are not Christians at all. Remember the words of our Lord:

Matthew 7:22, 23 – Many will say to Me on that day, 'Lord, Lord, did we not prophesy in Your name, and in Your name cast out demons, and in Your name perform many miracles?' And then I will declare to them, 'I never knew you; DEPART FROM ME, YOU WHO PRACTICE LAWLESSNESS.'

I leave it to the Lord to deal with all the phoniness, deceitfulness and pride that has been exhibited in this area of divine healing. But let's remind ourselves of this. Phony things from humans or deceptive things from Satan do not negate the miraculous power of God that He wants to perform for us through His Holy Spirit. As my mother used to say to me, "Don't throw out the baby with the bathwater." Let's look at some manifestations of the gifts of healings.

Consider three quick healing citations from the book of Acts. Acts 3:1-10 records Peter and John involved in the healing of the lame man. Acts 8:7 records many paralyzed and lame people being healed in Samaria, under the ministry of Philip. Acts 9:33, 34 tells the story of Aeneas of Lydda, who had been paralyzed and bedridden for eight years; Peter ministered to him and he was healed. As a result of each of these divine healings, many people became Christians. Signs and wonders were performed by the hand of God, as men proclaimed the gospel of the Lord Jesus Christ and it was evangelistic: many came to the Lord.

Now some present day manifestations of the gifts of healings. In the late 70's I was an associate pastor at an independent Pentecostal church in Seattle. I had a close relationship with the members of the congregation, and it was a time when God was teaching me about the believer's authority in prayer, the covering responsibility of leaders, fathers and husbands, and the importance of using our imagination for specific prayer requests. On one Saturday morning we were having a men's prayer meeting at church. One of the fathers shared a touching, emotional prayer request. He and his wife had recently adopted a wonderful Korean baby, just a few weeks old. The baby was having health problems, and was diagnosed with a dangerous heart condition. There was a significant hole between two of the baby's heart chambers, resulting in serious leakage and circulation weakness. If the baby was to live, he would require serious open-heart surgery, a very risky procedure for such a young one. I led in prayer asking for the Lord to touch the baby and heal him. As we were praying, I was directed of the Lord to have the father pray. I told him to pray and express what he wanted the Lord to do. I told him to picture exactly what he wanted to have happen, and to speak it out loud in his prayer request. He began praying, at first slowly, quietly and stumbling. But he suddenly took off. He began describing what the "hole" in his baby's heart was, and what was needed for it to close and disappear. It was obvious that the doctors had given him a clear picture of the problem, because he was very descriptive and specific in expressing his request to the Lord. It was powerful, and we all knew something had happened! In the following week, at an appointment with the surgeon, as they listened to the baby's heart, something had changed. Further tests were ordered, and finally the doctor came back to the couple. He couldn't explain it, but the baby's heart was normal, and had no hole or malformation. The heart was strong, the baby was healthy, and that was that! The gifts of healings came out of a men's prayer meeting and a father's heartfelt prayer.

Around that same time, a young married couple had come to me with tearful hearts. Although the wife was in her early twenties, she had been diagnosed with uterine cancer, and the doctors wanted to perform a full hysterectomy. They had not started a family yet, and they were scared, disappointed and fearful. As the three of us began praying together, the Lord directed me to have the husband speak out a leading prayer, as the spiritual covering for his wife, and to make his request for healing very detailed and specific. He did just that, asking for the cancer to be removed and for the uterus to be fresh and brand new tissue. We ended the prayer with a feeling of comfort and peace in the Lord. During the following week in a follow-up visit with the doctor, he noticed a difference in the uterine tissue, and took further samples to be sent to the lab. The result came back: no cancer! The doctor noticed that the tissue lining of the uterus was deep, fresh and healthy. I am happy to say that this couple had their first child in the next year. The gifts of healings came out of a "two-or-three" prayer time and a husband's leading prayer.

One day as my wife and I were working in the church office, one of the women of the congregation called, frantic about her husband. Something had happened to his back, and he was on the living room floor in intense pain and unable to move. She wanted us to come quickly and pray. My wife still had work to do for the pastor, so I grabbed a young man who happened to be at the church that day, and we went over to their home. I am a believer in the laying on of hands, but when a man is flat on his back on the floor, in tears from the pain, he doesn't need a bunch of hands touching him. I reached down, touched one shoulder, and we all began to pray. At that time in my life, I didn't know a lot about the spinal column, so I just asked God to do whatever was needed to heal him and stop the pain. I will say that all of us were emotionally intense as we prayed for his healing, calling on the name of the Lord Jesus Christ; and God answered. Suddenly he got up from the floor on his own. There was no more pain and he could move freely: no soreness, no ache, no pain. The Lord healed him, no ambulance was needed. He was one very happy man. The gifts of healings came out of a "two-or-three" prayer petition expressed in agreement with a wife's anxious plea.

GIFTS OF HEALING

A few years later I was part of another charismatic church in Seattle. It was a solid church with a great group of leading elders, and wonderful teaching. An older woman in the congregation had been hospitalized with cancer. It had not been contained and was spreading through her body. They were doing treatments, but the prognosis was terminal. We had prayer for her, again and again. The pastor would lead the congregation in prayer for her to be healed. Different teams would visit her hospital room to visit and pray for her healing. The elders visited, anointed her with oil and prayed for her healing. I personally visited her and prayed for her to be healed. My wife and two other ladies went as a team and prayed for her healing. An evangelist on our staff visited her and prayed for her to be healed. One Sunday morning our pastor announced that she had been released from the hospital,...and she had no cancer anywhere in her body. She was completely healed! In the next few years she continued to be part of that church, and cancer free. Now this is important for me to help you understand. Even though there were countless prayer efforts on her behalf, there was no one time when any assurance or revelation came from God that she was healed. Which prayer brought the healing? Who had the gifts of healings for her to be healed? Who was the faith healer in our midst? I believe it was all the prayers, each and every one, that God heard and responded to. What about the treatments the doctors were performing? Yes, there were chemical and radiation treatments, but it did not seem to be helping. And then, one day the scans showed everything clear...cancer free. The gifts of healings came out of many, many prayers; from individuals to a full congregation; from pastors and elders to congregational members.

Let's talk about my own disabilities for a moment. Back in 1970, I was shot in combat, and had damage to the nerves and muscles of my right leg. Over the next five years, with the help of physical therapy and crutches, canes and braces, I recovered to the point where I could walk and jog without any help. I did have a funny walk (doctors called it an abnormal gait). There were times I would pray for God to intervene and supernaturally heal me. But it did not happen. Doctors did tell me that it would probably get worse as I got older. My abnormal gait did have an effect, and in 2003 I had a severe impact on my lower back and the nerves of both of my legs. Degenerative disk disease in my lower back was impacting all the leg nerves. I could only move around with a walker. Over the next many years I had several surgeries to try to stop the deterioration in my health and bring improvement. Today I have twelve fused disks in my back (T5 – L5), and I live with pain and weakness of muscles and nerves in my back and legs. I can take a few steps with the aid of a cane, but for most short distances I use a walker. For longer distances I have a power wheelchair, provided by the V.A., and a lightweight mobility scooter if I have to fly somewhere. When I have the opportunity to preach and teach in church, usually a couple of the brothers help me step up onto the platform, and I sit in a chair, because standing hurts. But I still love preaching for my Lord and I will do it until I die! Over the last eleven years I have prayed for God's miraculous healing. I want God to heal me, so that I can jog three miles each evening, like I could do thirty five years ago. I don't want to set any speed records; I just want to be healed to walk and jog again. I have prayed for myself; I have had family pray for me; I have had elders pray for me; I have had pastors pray for me; I have had whole congregations pray for me; I have had strangers pray for me. All of these prayers were asking for a supernatural healing. I want the gifts of healings to work in me. I have had improvements through the work of doctors, therapists and family members, but I have not received a supernatural healing. There is still nerve damage, weakness and pain. I am still believing for my supernatural healing; I know God can do it, and I know He will do it; but it has not happened yet. I don't know why I have not been healed, when I believe in divine healing, but I will keep praying and I will keep believing. I trust God.

I have had a few times where God has had me preach on His healing power and the creative use of our own imaginations to see what God wants to do with assurance and conviction. I have said to the Lord, "Why me, Lord? I'm not healed. How can I be an example for faith? I haven't received much explanation from the Lord. It's kind of like He says, "Just do it."

Hebrews 11:1 – Now faith is the assurance of things hoped for, the conviction of things not seen.

At the conclusion of those sermons, people have come forward to be prayed for, and some have received supernatural healing. It is a beautiful thing to see the gifts of healings really happening. But some have not been healed.

I have watched men of God hold special healing services and pray for whoever needed healing of sicknesses, diseases or infirmities. Some of the speakers were a bit too flamboyant and showy for me, but others were careful to handle all things decently and in order. Some people received instant supernatural healing; others were healed within the next few days. It is a glorious thing to see the gifts of healings really happening. But there were always some who were not healed. I remember Kathryn Kuhlman from years ago. She had a desire that I don't think she ever realized. She asked the Lord to give her one crusade before she died, in which every person was healed. I personally attended her Seattle crusade years ago. Many were healed, but some were not.

My wife and I have been involved in altar prayer teams over the years, and many people have asked for prayer to be healed. We have seen some receive miraculous healing; it is a wonderful thing to see the gifts of healings really happening. But some have not been healed.

In all the situations I described above some people were healed, but others were not. I want to see everyone receive the gifts of healings. Acts chapter five gives us a clear picture of the early church in Jerusalem. The report had gone out that people were being supernaturally healed. People began bringing all the sick into the city. They would lay them beside the road, hoping that Peter's shadow might fall on them and they would be healed. The extraordinary thing is recorded in verse sixteen:

Acts 5:16 – Also the people from the cities in the vicinity of Jerusalem were coming together, bringing people who were sick or afflicted with unclean spirits, and they were all being healed.

They were all being healed!

They were all being healed. They were all being healed! That's what I want to see. I do not know why some people aren't healed. I don't know why I have not yet been healed. And I really don't know why God has continued to impress upon me to preach, teach and minister about divine healing. But I do know that God can supernaturally heal; I do know that God does supernaturally heal; I do know that God knows why He wants me to minister healing messages and why God's wants His church to manifest the gifts of healings.

In concluding this discussion of the gifts of healings, let's remind ourselves: Physical healing does not stand alone. Physical healing is not as important as spiritual healing. Physical healing is not as important as psychical (soul) healing. Healing of the body is accompanied by more important healing of the soul and healing of the spirit. Since we are in these physical bodies, and we are in this physical world, our tendency is to dwell on the physical healing aspect. But the divine healing of our soul and spirit is the most important aspect of the gifts of healings.

Chapter Fifteen

PROPHECY

God speaking revelations to build up,
warn and comfort His people

Prophecy (Greek-to speak for another; to proclaim a divine revelation). Prophecy is a divinely inspired and anointed utterance in a known language that is a message from God. It either proclaims a present truth or predicts a future truth (forth telling or foretelling).

As we examine the gift of prophecy we see that it can be predictive of the future, as used by the prophet Agabus in the book of Acts.

Acts 11:28 – One of them named Agabus stood up and began to indicate by the Spirit that there would certainly be a great famine all over the world. And this took place in the reign of Claudius.

Acts 21:10, 11 – As we were staying there for some days, a prophet named Agabus came down from Judea. And coming to us, he took Paul's belt and bound his own feet and hands, and said, "This is what the Holy Spirit says: 'In this way the Jews at Jerusalem will bind the man who owns this belt and deliver him into the hands of the Gentiles.'"

Prophecy can also be proclaiming truths for present circumstances.

I Corinthians 14:3 – But one who prophesies speaks to men for edification and exhortation and consolation.

Although this "forth telling" may not be predictive of the future, it is important to the church that this form of prophecy also be shared. These words build people up, warn people and comfort people. The Holy Spirit knows the special times when a special word from Him will meet the needs of regular people. I have been used by God in the gift of prophecy for over thirty-five years. It has been a growing process, with a gradual learning curve. I look back over the years and see some times that the gift of prophecy that the Holy Spirit used through me had a wonderful, positive impact; and then sometimes I have fouled up the Holy Spirit's message by adding my own words or attitude. Let me give you some examples.

Back in the late 80's I was pastoring a church, and God gave me a prophecy for a young woman in our congregation. She was a single sister in her late 30's, who was leaving on a summer ministry trip; she was a group leader with Teen Missions. Whenever we had someone from our church going on a special ministry trip, we would call all the elders up and pray for them. We would send them out with our blessings. During that prayer time with the elders (this is referred to as the laying on of hands of the presbytery) God gave me a prophecy for her. It scared me because specific, predictive prophecies always scared me. What if I had just imagined it? What if I was wrong? But I spoke it anyway, because I was certain it was the Holy Spirit. The prophecy said that on this mission trip she would meet the man to whom she would become a "helpmeet." That's a King James word from Genesis chapter two, describing Eve as the only one found who was a helpmeet, or helper suitable for Adam. It meant that she would find the husband to whom she would become a wife in Christian marriage. And she would find him on this several week summer trip. Oh boy, by sharing that prophecy I had really stuck my neck out. What if it didn't happen? Well, she received the prophecy from me, and considered it. She didn't become obsessed with finding a man and she didn't let it distract her from ministering to the teens she was leading in a work project. The team of leaders had some from the U.S. and some from Australia. To make a long story short, she developed a friendship, then a relationship with a man from Australia. They became engaged about six months later, and then after a year, he came to the United States for a couple of months to join his fiancée and go through pre-marital counseling with me. I had the privilege of performing the wedding ceremony for them, and a few months later they moved to Australia. They had a wonderful marriage, a great ministry together, and the prophecy was fulfilled, exactly as it had been given by the Holy Spirit through me. That was an excellent manifestation of the gift of prophecy.

My thoughts, emotions and will polluted the pure prophetic word of God.

Another time I was pastoring a church in which we were growing in the strength of our prayer times together. The pre-service prayer time had become powerful in preparing our hearts to receive from the Word and minister to one another. Well, there came a week I had been away at a Minister's Conference. In order to get home in time to preach in the

Sunday morning service, I took a red-eye flight home. There's a reason they call it a red eye flight: you don't get to sleep. I do not sleep well, if at all on airplanes, so I arrived in my home town just before Sunday Services, exhausted, but still determined to preach and lead the service. In the pre-service prayer I could tell the Holy Spirit was stirring my heart to prophesy. It was a prophecy of exhortation to seek the face of God, and to draw near to Him. I also noticed that few of the people had participated in our pre-service prayer time, and I was annoyed by that. When the service started there came a time for gifts of the Spirit to be shared, and I proceeded to minister my prophecy. I call it my prophecy because two things went very wrong. 1- I was physically exhausted and that was affecting my soul and spirit. 2- I was annoyed at the conduct of God's people. The bottom line is that my thoughts, emotions and will polluted the pure prophetic word of God. What I spoke was harsh and rebuking, and it hurt the hearts of God's people. That is an excellent example of how a Christian's soul can twist and pollute the precious gift of prophecy. Over the years I have vowed that if I am tired or exhausted, I will not speak a prophecy polluted by my soul. I have said more than once in my teachings: if you've just come into town on a red eye, don't be prophesying.

Romans 12:6 – Since we have gifts that differ according to the grace given to us, each of us is to exercise them accordingly: if prophecy, according to the proportion of his faith;

When a person prophesies, they are to do it according to the proportion of their faith. The "proportion" is a unique Greek word that refers to a mathematical measure or amount. It is saying that people grow in wisdom and experience, and subsequently their measure or amount increases in the kind of faith that allows for Holy Spirit exactness, not affected by their

PROPHECY

own human feelings, thoughts and will. Let me cite a Biblical progression that shows this.

Please take the time to read Acts chapters 19, 20 and 21. Look at the story of Paul returning from Ephesus to Jerusalem at the end of his third missionary journey. I want to highlight several verses:

Acts 19:21 – Now after these things were finished, Paul purposed in the Spirit to go to Jerusalem after he had passed through Macedonia and Achaia, saying, "After I have been there, I must also see Rome."

While in Ephesus, Paul purposed in the Spirit to go to Jerusalem. "Purposed in the Spirit" means that this mighty man of God sensed what the Spirit wanted to happen, and he purposed to do it. This is the measure and amount of faith that an experienced apostle exercises when the Spirit lays a message on his spirit.

Acts 20: 22, 23 – And now, behold, bound by the Spirit, I am on my way to Jerusalem, not knowing what will happen to me there, except that the Holy Spirit solemnly testifies to me in every city, saying that bonds and afflictions await me.

While in Miletus, Paul was addressing the Ephesians elders. Paul said he was bound by the Spirit, on his way to Jerusalem. He said that the Holy Spirit was solemnly testifying to him in every city, that bonds and afflictions awaited him in Jerusalem. But that's where he was going. This is the measure and amount of faith that an experienced apostle exercises when the Spirit lays a message on his spirit.

Acts 21:4 – After looking up the disciples, we stayed there seven days; and they kept telling Paul through the Spirit not to set foot in Jerusalem.

While in Tyre, Paul and his party were staying with the disciples, and they told him through the Spirit not to set foot in

Jerusalem. They were sensing something from the Spirit and they decided that it must mean that Paul should not set foot in Jerusalem. They kept telling him that "through the Spirit." That probably means that they were saying something like this: "Paul, the Holy Spirit has told us that you shouldn't go to Jerusalem." This contradicted what Paul knew the Holy Spirit wanted. This is the measure and amount of faith that inexperienced disciples can exercise when the Spirit touches them with a message.

Acts 21:9 – Now this man (Philip the evangelist) had four virgin daughters who were prophetesses (literally "who did prophesy").

In Caesarea, Philip's four virgin daughters were known for exercising the gift of prophecy. They weren't prophetesses, but they were used in prophecy a lot. I would say that they were used in the gift of prophecy more frequently and accurately than the other Christians in the church. That's what they were known for: prophesying. Interestingly enough they did not say anything with regard to the issue of Paul going to Jerusalem. They undoubtedly had a larger measure and amount of faith than other inexperienced Christians. Yet the Holy Spirit did not use them in prophecy to settle this issue.

Acts 21:10, 11 – a prophet named Agabus came down from Judea. And coming to us, he took Paul's belt and bound his own feet and hands, and said, "This is what the Holy Spirit says, 'In this way the Jews at Jerusalem will bind the man who owns this belt and deliver him into the hands of the Gentiles.'"

In Caesarea, the prophet Agabus gave a visual demonstration and said exactly what the Holy Spirit said. He spoke out of the larger measure and amount of faith that he had. With the wisdom and experience of a prophet, he could speak the exact words of the Holy Spirit, without the affects of human feelings, thoughts and will. This is what I strive for in ministering the gift of prophecy.

Acts 21:12 – When we had heard this, we as well as the local residents began begging him (Paul) not to go up to Jerusalem.

Acts 21:14 – And when he (Paul) would not be persuaded, we fell silent, remarking, "The will of the Lord be done."

Now follow this. A prophet had just spoken the exact words of the Holy Spirit, and the local Christians and the members of Paul's own party (including Luke) began begging him not to go to Jerusalem. They had thoughts and feelings about him being imprisoned and they made their decision on what should happen based on that, instead of the exact words of the Holy Spirit. Paul outlined for them what was happening, how the Holy Spirit knew what was going to happen, and still was guiding him to go to Jerusalem. They all then concluded that it must be God's will for him to go. I point this out because they were telling Paul what to do without really knowing God's will. None of the people in Acts chapters 19, 20 and 21 were wicked or evil; but many of them were mistaken about what the Holy Spirit was saying and what He wanted. They let their feelings and wants affect how they interpreted the impressions and words of the Holy Spirit.

Through His gifts the Holy Spirit spoke multiple times to Christians (including Paul) about Paul's ministry and trip to Jerusalem. Christian leaders, missionaries, and even Luke himself, applied what the Holy Spirit said in the wrong way – they made mistakes and were speaking out contrary to the plan of God. The prophet Agabus, who had knowledge, training and experience, and had a greater measure and amount of faith, communicated the words of the Holy Spirit, without diluting it with his own feelings, thoughts, opinions or desires. Agabus prophesied according to the proportion of his faith.

Christians with the best of intentions can dilute or misapply the Holy Spirit's words and giftings.

Christians with the best of intentions can dilute or misapply the Holy Spirit's words and giftings. We want to be used by the Holy Spirit in the gift of prophecy, and avoid making mistakes. Let's get knowledge, training and experience, in order to do it right, to glorify God and not distract from His perfect approach, and to win people the way the Holy Spirit wants to do it. There are prophets, there are people used frequently in the gift of prophecy and there are people who sense the Holy Spirit and get spiritual inclinations. These all have different measures and amounts of faith, according to the grace given them by God. Let's be careful, wise and sensitive.

In the past thirty-five years I have heard a lot of prophecies and a lot of people prophesying. We have sometimes built it up into quite a show. Speaking about myself and many other people who have prophesied, we have added a lot of our own thoughts, feelings and wants to whatever it was that the Spirit of God gave us to prophesy. That's not good. I liken what we would do to a short airplane trip. We had particular words and phrases that we used for the take off (Thus saith the Spirit of God…The Lord would say…Hear now the word of God…and so on). When we had finally taken off, then we would speak the words of the Holy Spirit (that's the prophecy). Then we would bring it in for a landing. The problem is that all the take-off and landing words were not the prophecy. Those words were just our staging, our thoughts, our feelings. We who are used in the gift of prophecy need to stop all the stuff that is "us," and try to speak only the words that are Holy Spirit words. Before I speak prophecy, I cry out to God: "Please Lord, none of me and all of you!" If every Christian who exercised the gift of prophecy would say this prayer and have this heart before the Lord, then we would truly see Holy Spirit edification, exhortation and consolation. That's the gift of prophecy and it's great!

Prophecy can be directed to the whole group, or to individuals. I believe that personal prophecy is a valuable tool that the Holy Spirit uses to bring His spoken word to individuals. But it needs careful consideration and covering. If someone tries to direct and control you with personal prophecy, be careful. Ask the Holy Spirit to give you confirmation or check. Ask the counsel of your pastor/spiritual leader. If it is really the Holy Spirit's word, then you will get positive confirmation. If you are used by God to speak personal prophecy to someone, speak it with careful humility. If possible have their pastor or other spiritual leaders present, so that the word may be judged. When I speak of pastors, other elders or spiritual leaders, I am talking about spiritual covering. It is the Lone Ranger prophet who is not covered, or does not submit to spiritual authority covering, that does damage to Christians. I have seen "personal prophecy" abused by individuals who like to control others. Don't do it,...and don't let it happen to you!

One more thing: prophecy is a divine utterance. That means it is God's words, not man's words. Some translations and paraphrases have used the word "preaching" in place of the word "prophecy." I remember as a teenager back in the 60's, I first encountered Bible paraphrases, and I really appreciated how they helped me understand the Bible better. But even as a teenager, when I saw that the most popular paraphrases translated the word prophecy as preaching, I knew that couldn't be right. I knew preachers preached good messages about the Bible. But I also knew that prophecy was something special from the Holy Spirit. I still know that today; after studying Greek in Bible college, I can tell you that the Greek words for preaching and prophesying are two very different words. Make no mistake: prophecy is not any one man's message; rather it is the divine message of the Holy Spirit. That's the gift of prophecy, and I say it again: it's great!

Chapter Sixteen

DISTINGUISHING OF SPIRITS

God helping His people to know spirits and act accordingly

Distinguishing of spirits (Greek – distinguishing, differentiating). Distinguishing of spirits is a supernatural gift from the Holy Spirit that allows a Christian believer to determine what spirit is behind any action or person: a good spirit (angel, Holy Spirit), an evil spirit (demons, Satan), a human spirit. It does not refer to whether an individual person's spirit or motives are good or bad; right or wrong. We're talking spirits here: human spirits, angels, demons, the Holy Spirit or Satan.

The single biggest mistake I have seen over the years with regard to this gift is the seeming application of discernment to motives. Again and again I have heard people say something like this: "I discern that your motives are wrong. You're doing this thing because your motives are…" Most of the time as I have heard what people had to say about someone else's motives, it has revealed that they haven't received anything from the Holy Spirit. They are expressing their own opinions, and often trying to control other people by declaring God's name: "The Holy Spirit has given me a word of discernment that you are wrong in your motives, and you need to change." It is a sad thing when someone declares that something is from the Holy Spirit, is from God, when it's really just their own thoughts and will. That is a violation of the commandment:

Exodus 20:7 – You shall not take the name of the LORD your God in vain, for the LORD will not leave him unpunished who takes His name in vain.

If someone starts to judge your motives and cites the gift of discernment from the Holy Spirit, get your guard up because that's not the Holy Spirit.

This gift is the help that the Holy Spirit gives us to distinguish or differentiate what spirit is behind something.

One of the ways that God uses this gift for us is in the recognition of demon possession. We have a broad spectrum of views in the Christian community on this particular issue. There are those who don't believe in demon possession at all; then there are those who believe that many people are demon possessed: both Christians and non-Christians. Demon possession refers to the condition in which Satan or a demon gets inside of a person and forces them to do something. It is not just an influence; Satan or a demon compromises the individual's free will and makes them do something. We do see several situations of demon possession described in the gospels, but we also see that most people were not demon possessed.

Back in the late 70's the comedy world enjoyed the antics of Flip Wilson. He made one phrase very popular: "the devil made me do it." Whatever comedy routine he was involved in, there always came a point where he did something wrong or bad; then he would suddenly pop up with the excuse: "the devil made me do it." It was funny and it always got a laugh. Everybody would laugh because it was ridiculously funny to blame one's bad conduct on the devil. Everyone really knew that you couldn't blame the devil for making you do something. You were responsible for your own actions. Well, around that same time I was ministering in the Seattle area and encountering a large number of charismatics who were practicing casting out demons. But this had a unique twist: they were casting demons out of one another. There were times that they would encounter a sin problem in their life or in one of their friend's lives, and they would blame it on a demon, and would cast the demon out! What was especially interesting to me is that getting the demon cast out did not last for long. They would have to go back to the same person and situation and cast out the demon again and again. They actually told me that sometimes the casting out of the demon wouldn't last long, and they would have to repeat the process three or four times. These were Christians practicing casting demons out of one another, again and again! As a pastor, I could see that these spiritual, charismatic Christians were using this practice to avoid taking responsibility for their own actions. Even non-Christians knew it was a silly joke to blame the devil. While Satan or a demon can deceive, trick and trap a Christian, they can't possess a Christian and force him to do something against his will. God is inside every Christian; therefore a demon can't be in there at the same time.

Suddenly God's Spirit let me know that it was a demon in the young man.

In the last forty-five years, I have only encountered a legitimate case of demon possession three or four times. As I recall, in one situation, I was in a room of with four teenagers. They had skipped school and come into our church building, probably to do some mischief. I surprised them, and they tried to bluff it through by saying they were looking for a pastor to talk to. But I took the opportunity to share the real message of salvation. A couple of them were listening, and I could tell that they were close to receiving Jesus Christ. One young man in particular was persistently interrupting and contradicting me. It was distracting all of us from the crucial decision of accepting Jesus Christ. I was arguing with him when suddenly God's Spirit let me know that it was a demon in the young man who was speaking and resisting me. I spoke out boldly, addressing the demon: "Be silent in the name of the Lord Jesus Christ." The young man suddenly fled from the room. I turned again to the other young people, and one girl prayed with me to accept Jesus Christ. This was absolutely the Holy Spirit exercising the gift of discerning of spirits in me, so that I would quit the futile argument with the young man, and instead silence the demon that was really behind the whole resistance. One young lady's salvation was in the balance.

I remember another time when a young man who was part of a family in the church was brought to me by his sister for prayer. He was not a Christian, and was struggling with drinking, drugs and illicit sex. He was obviously reluctant to be prayed for. As I began to pray for him, the Holy Spirit immediately told me he was possessed by a demon. I spoke to the demon in the name of the Lord Jesus Christ and commanded him to come out of the young man. The demon spoke back, but I silenced him and commanded again that he come out of him in the name of the Lord Jesus Christ. With a convulsive shudder the young man suddenly went limp, and then slowly opened his eyes. I knew that the demon was gone and spoke the gospel to the young man so that he could immediately become a Christian. "Will you pray with me now to accept Jesus into your life?" I was amazed when he answered me: "I'm not ready; I have to think about it." I explained to him that a demon had been controlling him and he needed God's protection for that not to happen again.

Matthew 12:43-45 – "Now when the unclean spirit goes out of a man, it passes through waterless places seeking rest, and does not find it. Then it says, 'I will return to my house from which I came'; and when it comes, it finds it unoccupied, swept, and put in order. Then it goes and takes along with it seven other spirits more wicked than itself, and they go in and live there; and the last state of that man becomes worse than the first. That is the way it will also be with this evil generation."

If a demon is cast out of someone, they need to be "occupied" to prevent the demon from returning. The only 100% guarantee of not having a demon possess you is to accept Jesus Christ as your Savior and Lord. At the moment of salvation God comes to live inside of you, and a demon cannot live inside of you again because God is greater. I explained this to the young man and pleaded with him to accept Jesus, but he just kept saying, "I'm not ready." I couldn't believe it! I know that every story we tell about casting demons out is supposed to have a happy ending, but this one did not. I tried to contact him after that, but he wouldn't see me again. I prayed a lot for him, but he did not come to the Lord that I knew of. This was another example of the Holy Spirit using the gift of distinguishing of spirits in me and in my ministry. If I had not known the evil spirit was inside the young man, I could have spent hours trying to talk to him and figure out what needed to be done. Thank the Holy Spirit for the gift of distinguishing of spirits.

Now, suppose you are in an elders meeting, and there is discussion as to whether the church should move into a new area of ministry. Some of the elders want to move forward, while others are not certain that it is what God wants.

Obviously all of the elders want to do what God wants, but sometimes it takes time to sort out what God wants to do and when He wants to do it. Then one of the elders speaks up and says, "The Holy Spirit wants us to move in faith and begin this ministry right away." I have seen this very thing happen in an elders meeting. For most of the other elders they automatically take this as a word from God, and want to vote in favor of doing it. As a pastor leading an elders meeting I want to be aware always of what the Holy Spirit is doing, so that I can judge any and all gifts properly. God has been faithful to help me in these kinds of situations. God has shown me when something is coming from His Spirit, or from the spirit of a man. Consequently I have been able to speak up and say, "I appreciate your conviction in sharing this word, but I believe that is coming from your own spirit and desires, and not necessarily from the Holy Spirit. Are you sure you are expressing what the Holy Spirit wants, or are you expressing your own personal spirit and desire?" The elder has then backed off his declaration of what the Holy Spirit wants. Notice that I did not rebuke or silence the elder. Thoughtful wording and communication allows Christian brothers and sisters to have discussion without getting defensive. For me as a pastor leading an elders meeting, this example shows the Holy Spirit exercising the gift of distinguishing of spirits in me. I have also had it happen, where an elder has shared a word from the Lord regarding an issue or decision, and the Holy Spirit has immediately confirmed in my heart that the elder is speaking the word of the Lord. Remember that the gift of distinguishing of spirits will also help us perceive the Holy Spirit.

Chapter Seventeen

FINAL PRINCIPLES OF PRACTICE FOR THE GIFTS

Regular people successfully exercising
Holy Spirit ministry gifts

About the rest. I'm not discussing in depth the remaining four gifts of the Spirit, as set forth in I Corinthians 12:8-10, except to give the following definitions. I believe all the previous things we have discussed should equip you with wise principles and practices to successfully function in all of the gifts.

Gift of faith (Greek-faith) – This gift is a supernaturally bestowed faith that overcomes obstacles and works wonders. This is not saving faith; it is not the measure of faith each Christian is given by God. It is a special gift of faith given to certain individuals in order for them to operate in total faith/belief in a given situation.

Effecting of miracles (Greek-workings or operations of power, deeds of power, miracles, wonders) – The effecting of miracles allows the gifted one to exercise supernatural power to perform miracles. Miracles are an intervention of God into the regular operation of things. God supernaturally suspends the laws of nature.

Speaking in tongues (Greek-kinds of tongues) – This gift is a supernatural utterance from the Holy Spirit, in a language (heavenly or earthly) unknown to the speaker. It may be addressed to God or to men.

Interpretation of tongues (Greek-translation/interpretation of tongues) – This gift is a supernatural utterance in a language known to the speaker and audience. It translates the gift of speaking in tongues.

Final Principles. Being a preacher, I have found that I can come up with really long lists. Reviewing my teachings from the last 40 years, I could go on and on and on with rules and principles about using the gifts of the Spirit. Fortunately the Lord has helped me melt all that down to six pearls that will help every Christian exercise the ministry gifts of the Spirit with success. Success is defined as acting in such a way that you accomplish what God wants to have done. I am expressing these statements to the singular "you," because I want each one of us to think about it personally. But the statements apply to each and every Christian. Please apply and practice these pearls.

1. **God entrusts you with gifts. That means He trusts you!** This is a great confidence builder for every one of us. When we look at ourselves, we see our weaknesses, sins and failures, and we don't feel qualified to exercise spiritual gifts. But God, who knows us better than we know ourselves, and sees our weaknesses, sins and failures, and even sees what we do in the future, still entrusts us with His supernatural gifts. Satan would like nothing better than to see us choosing not to exercise ministry gifts because of self-condemna-

FINAL PRINCIPLES OF PRACTICE FOR THE GIFTS

tion. Satan is always around with condemnation, and his goal is to get us to quit: quit ministering, quit trusting God, quit being Christians, quit living. But God trusts you and me! If He is willing to entrust to you His precious gifts, that means He trusts you.

2. **You are all that, but you aren't all that.** I'm not just trying to be funny, but it does seem to me that a lot of Christians either fail to see how tremendous they are, or think of themselves way too highly. Neither position is correct.

II Corinthians 5:21 – He made Him who knew no sin to be sin on our behalf, so that we might become the righteousness of God in Him.

Every Christian is the righteousness of God in Christ Jesus. Every Christian is a righteous person, not based on their own good works, but based on the work of Jesus on the cross. So you are all that, thanks to Jesus. That means you are qualified to minister the gifts of the Spirit.

Romans 12:3 – For through the grace given to me I say to everyone among you not to think more highly of himself than he ought to think; but to think so as to have sound judgment, as God has allotted to each a measure of faith.

But as you minister the gifts, and you get better and better at it, and more and more people are blessed, don't get cocky. After a tremendous prophecy, after a supernatural healing, after a key word of wisdom, after guiding the group into the perfect will of the Holy Spirit, you're still a Christian, saved by grace. Don't get cocky. You don't have "healing hands or "gold dust" on your fingers. You may be God's gift to the church, but you're not special because of that. Stay humble. God is opposed to the proud, but gives grace to the humble.

What is it about so many Christians that they like to put on a show?

3. **Don't put on a show; just love, serve and pray.** What is it about so many Christians that they like to put on a show? Let's stop all the nonsense. In carefulness, decency, orderliness and under the covering and authority of our spiritual leaders, let's love people, serve people and pray for people. We don't see healing crusades or special personal prophecy services in the Bible; what we see are regular people sharing their personal testimonies of the gospel. As the gospel was shared and people got together, ministry gifts were exercised in the spiritual course of things. Although Apollos was eloquent in speech, people weren't trained to speak in special ways to stir people's faith. Sounds and lights and staging weren't necessary to have the gifts of the Spirit ministered. If you are to be used by the Holy Spirit in ministering one of His gifts, don't be a showman! Thirty-three years ago I was a staff pastor in Seattle, and I remember catching myself halfway through a sermon, declaring the name of Jesus by saying something like this: "And Jeaaaaasus! will heal you!" Maybe I had been listening to too many Christian T.V. Crusades, or maybe I was just feeling my oats. After the service, my senior pastor talked to me

FINAL PRINCIPLES OF PRACTICE FOR THE GIFTS

about toning down some of my "southern twang" preaching. He was right, of course. It's so easy for us to put on a show. As each one of us try to allow the pure ministry of the Holy Spirit, remember our heart's cry should be: "More of you, Holy Spirit, and less of me." The Holy Spirit does not need our showmanship.

4. **A team works better (two or three).** Over the last many years, when I have seen excesses or errors in the ministry of the gifts of the Holy Spirit, it has been mostly by individuals, acting alone. I remember one lady named Helen, who regularly spoke personal prophecy to others. She had a dominating influence over one particular single sister, and it all revolved around her speaking personal prophecies in private to the individual. When they came into our congregation, I instructed them both on what to do if a personal prophecy was to be spoken: call me, and share it with the individual in front of me, so that I could judge it, as is taught in I Corinthians 14:29. Two things immediately happened: Helen didn't seem to get personal prophecies anymore, and the other single sister began to blossom in her relationship with the Lord and with the rest of the congregation. Helen soon moved on to some other church. Her dominating kind of personal prophecy would not stand up to judgment, and going to a "two or three" approach revealed this and protected God's people.

By the same token when I have seen correct and strong ministry of the gifts of the Holy Spirit, it has been done mostly by a team or a group working together.

Matthew 9:19 – "Again I say to you, that if two of you agree on earth about anything that they may ask, it shall be done for them by My Father who is in heaven. For where two or three have gathered together in My name, I am there in their midst.

I have had the joy and fulfillment of being used in many of the gifts of the Spirit over the years: the word of wisdom, the word of knowledge, faith, gifts of healing, prophecy, distinguishing of spirits, and tongues. In almost every situation, I have worked with a team: a group of elders, a prayer group, a prayer team, a pastor and prophet team and a husband-wife team with my own wife. It has always worked for the best in this way. Jesus Himself, in introducing us to the "two or three" principle, laid out the essential pattern for every function and ministry in the church. The pattern is expressed in three words: together, agreement, unity. When we come together with two or three or more, we can then move into agreement about whatever, and our prayers and actions bring us into unity. When my pastor prays for people, and speaks prophecy over them, I often stand beside him and the Holy Spirit has me speak a word of wisdom or knowledge that blends perfectly with the prophecy and brings a really complete picture to whomever is being prayed for. When I and my wife are praying for people that have come forward at the end of the service, our prayers, words of knowledge, words of wisdom and prophecy blend together to accomplish exactly what the Holy Spirit desires. And I have noticed that when we are praying for a couple, the couple just seems to open up to the Holy Spirit when this team ministry occurs. Upon occasion the Holy Spirit has given me a strong or hard-hitting prophecy or word to speak over someone. I ask for another elder or pastor to pray with me over the individual. I want them there for the sake of the individual; they add consideration, judgment,

FINAL PRINCIPLES OF PRACTICE FOR THE GIFTS

counsel or whatever is needed. This is the great way to have authority and covering available to protect the individual from error. When you minister a gift of the Holy Spirit, do it as part of a team. That's the Bible pattern that Jesus taught us.

> **People have grown skeptical and fearful of people who call themselves prophets.**

5. **Acknowledge God: His gift, your ministry.** In this day and age, semantics are not as important to the common person as they once were. So there are prophets today, because Jesus Christ continues giving prophets to mankind, as spoken of in Ephesians 4:11. But because a lot of people have grown skeptical and fearful of people who call themselves prophets, most of God's prophets today are happy just being called ministers or pastors, who have a strong prophetic gift. If God gives the church a prophet, and the church calls him a pastor with a strong prophetic gift, as long as he still ministers in the Holy Spirit, the will of the Lord will be accomplished. So the Lord continues to teach me that He is not as hung up on semantics (what you call something) as I am. Mellow out, Reed. But who is acknowledged is important. I exhort every Christian to first acknowledge God before you minister a gift. It is a gift of the Holy Spirit; He provides and empowers the gift, while you serve by performing the ministry. Every time you minister a gift of the Spirit, start by

acknowledging that it is God's power and gift. Then humbly love, pray and serve.

6. **Encourage oversight, covering and counsel.** When you minister a powerful personal prophecy to someone, they are often encouraged, excited and raring to take action. Whatever the gift is that you minister, start and end by encouraging the individual to seek counsel from his leadership. Whatever the gift is that you minister, make sure that your leadership covering knows about it. If possible they should be present when you minister. The Body of Christ runs on effective oversight, protective covering and shepherding counsel.

And please be subject to your covering and oversight. If you find yourself not wanting to hear input from your pastor or elder about your ministry, watch out! You may be becoming too confident in self, and not as teachable because of pride. When it all comes down to it, ministry is service, and service is being a slave. We like to use semantics that make us sound like somebody special, but when it's all said and done we are slaves of the Lord Jesus Christ. Encourage individuals that you minister to, to look to their oversight and covering for counsel. And keep yourself humble and submitted to your own oversight and covering for counsel. That's the Holy Spirit way.

Please apply and practice these pearls and reap successful results from the ministry gifts of the Holy Spirit.

IN CLOSING

When you and I became Christians, we accepted Jesus Christ as our Savior and Lord. From that moment on God came to dwell inside of us by His Holy Spirit. If you aren't a Christian, or you're not sure if you are a Christian, let's take care of that right now. Pray with me:

"Dear Lord, I confess that I am a sinner. I have done wrong things in my life. Please forgive me for my sins. I believe that you are the son of God, and that you died on the cross to pay for my sins, and to bring me salvation. I accept you as my Savior and Lord, and I turn my life over to you. Come sit on the throne of my heart and help me live an abundant life. I love you and I thank you."

If you prayed that sincerely between you and the Lord you are a Christian, your sins are forgiven and God is dwelling inside of you. In this book we have talked about the Holy Spirit a lot, but make no mistake, God is one in three and three in one. He is the Father and the Son and the Holy Spirit: He is the Lord Jesus Christ, and He is inside of you. The Father and the Son are not separated from the Holy Spirit, off somewhere in the heavens. Neither is the Holy Spirit separated from the Father and the Son, inside of you but away from Them. All of God is inside of you and also everywhere.

The first connection I always teach for new converts and new additions is this concept of the indwelling of God. You and I need to connect to God inside of us. The catechism I use to teach this concept is very simple:

Question: Where is God?

Answer:
Inside of me, and also everywhere.

As my pastor is fond of saying to the congregation: "If you are a Christian, you have a ghost inside of you: the Holy Ghost, the Holy Spirit. He is your Comforter and Spirit of Truth. It is difficult for us to understand having God inside of us, but it is true and it is vital to our functioning in the Holy Spirit. It is not magic, and even though we can't comprehend it, we can embrace the experience and enjoy the full benefits. He is our personal Savior and Lord, and as we walk the Christian path, it is crucial that we conduct ourselves in awareness. God is inside of each of us all the time, twenty-four hours a day. It is critical that we practice this truth by becoming aware of His presence inside of us. Once we are aware of His presence within we can appropriate His baptism and His gifting. By appropriate I mean use the guidance and gifting that the Holy Spirit gives to each of us, in power and in truth.

I ask you to set aside whatever traditions, presuppositions or prejudices that you may have that could separate you from the truth of God's Word. Walk in the fullness of the Holy Spirit; be baptized with the Holy Spirit; be strengthened by the gift of speaking in tongues; be used in the ministry gifts of the Spirit. This is God's plan for all of us, and that is my goal in sharing with you this Holy Ghost Primer.

ABOUT THE AUTHOR

Reed Tibbetts has served for over twenty-three years as an ordained pastor and teacher, and is currently serving as one of the elders of VLife Church in McKinney, Texas, where he ministers as a prophet and teacher.

An honored and decorated disabled veteran of the Vietnam War, Reed is a graduate of Northwest University of the Assemblies of God. Over the many years he has pursued the goal of handling accurately the word of truth, and has developed a reputation as a guardian of apostolic doctrine (the teachings of the apostles).

Through the years Reed has written and printed many teaching notebooks in the churches he has served, but only recently has he turned to the writing and publishing of books for the greater body of Christ.

Reed lives in Princeton, Texas with his wife of forty-six years. They have three adult children and four grandchildren, all of whom are faithfully serving the Lord in their respective local churches.

AUTHOR CONTACT

Reed has written several other books about the successful Christian life. If you would like to contact him, find out more information, purchase books, or request him to speak, please contact:

Allegro Ministries
470 San Remo
Princeton, TX 75407
yahovah3@gmail.com
214 724-7541

Allegro Ministries is a non-profit corporation, formed by Reed and his family, recognized as a 501(c)(3) by the I.R.S. It exists for the purpose of spreading relevant teachings to the church of the Lord Jesus Christ, so that more and more people can live the brisk and lively Christian walk. If you would like to contribute to the ministry, please send your offerings to the above address, and thank you for your giving.

www.ingramcontent.com/pod-product-compliance
Lightning Source LLC
LaVergne TN
LVHW051120080426
835510LV00018B/2154